AQA STUDY GUIDE

GCSE 9–1

LOVE AND RELATIONSHIPS

POETRY ANTHOLOGY

SCHOLASTIC

Authors Richard Durant and Cindy Torn

Reviewer Rob Pollard

Editorial team Rachel Morgan, Audrey Stokes, Lesley Densham, Louise Titley

Typesetting Jayne Rawlings/Oxford Raw Design

Cover design Dipa Mistry and Jason Cox

App development Hannah Barnett, Phil Crothers and RAIOSOFT International Pvt Ltd

Photographs
page 11: teardrop, LedyX/shutterstock; page 12: faded rose, Sasin Paraksa/Shutterstock; page 15: Himalayan mountain, Galyna Andrushko/Shutterstock; page 16: poppies entwined, elena moiseeva/Shutterstock; swirling water, 108MotionBG/ Shutterstock; page 20: painting by Sophie Gengembre Anderson, photographed by Art Renewal Centre; page 21: Robert Browning, duncan1890/iStock; lightning hitting tree, Sergey Nivens/Shutterstock; page 22: fiery lips, ShamanXIX/ Shutterstock; page 25: vine leaves, Chansom Pantip/ iStock; page 26: palm tree, DNY59/iStock; page 26 and 27: vine leaves, ArtisticPhoto/Shutterstock; page 29: snowy scene, AnettaNecia/iStock; page 30: leaves, NeagoneFo/ Shutterstock; page 33: planting potatoes, Elena Masiutkina/ Shutterstock; page 34: lapwing, Klaas Vledder/Shutterstock; page 35: hands, cunaplus/Shutterstock; page 38: woman with basket, ilbusca/iStock; wild hare, Simon Bratt/Shutterstock; keys, Africa Studio/Shutterstock; page 39: wedding rings, dencg/Shutterstock; farmhouse, Helen Hotson/Shutterstock; page 40: wild hare running, Volodymyr Burdiak/Shutterstock; page 41: bare tree, Vastram/Shutterstock; page 43: football player, cjp/iStock; page 44: sycamore seeds, joannawnuk/ Shutterstock; white lines on sports pitch, Thomas Reville/ Shutterstock; page 47: picnic by the lake, Everett Collection/ Shutterstock; page 48: stream, Giacomo Carlomagno/ Shutterstock; page 49: stone skimming, SteAck/Shutterstock; page 51: horse plough, Stephen Barnes/iStock; page 52: old man, silentalex88/Shutterstock; ship, iurii/Shutterstock; page 55: woman measuring, PHILIPIMAGE/Shutterstock; page 56: skylight, coki10/Shutterstock; page 56 and page 57: measuring tape, Oksana Mizina/Shutterstock; page 59 and page 61: women vintage collage, Lisa-Blue/iStock; page 60: red high heels, Oksana Kuzmina/Shutterstock; page 61: photo album, optimarc/Shutterstock; page 63: two white swans, ira_kalina/Shutterstock; page 64: two swans, Vova Shevchuk/ Shutterstock; page 68 and page 70: Indian Sikh man, Ranta Images/Shutterstock; page 69: grocery shop, I Wei Huang/ Shutterstock; page 73: child and grandfather's hand, Brilliant Eye/Shutterstock; page 74: child rock climbing, Maria Symchych/Shutterstock; page 84: girl sitting exam, Monkey Business Images/Shutterstock; page 85: notepad and pen, TRINACRIA PHOTO/Shutterstock

Designed using Adobe InDesign

Published in the UK by Scholastic Education, 2019
Book End, Range Road, Witney, Oxfordshire, OX29 0YD
A division of Scholastic Limited
London – New York – Toronto – Sydney – Auckland
Mexico City – New Delhi – Hong Kong
SCHOLASTIC and associated logos are trademarks and/or registered trademarks of Scholastic Inc.
www.scholastic.co.uk

1 2 3 4 5 6 7 8 9 9 0 1 2 3 4 5 6 7 8

British Library Cataloguing-in-Publication Data
A catalogue record for this book is available from the British Library.

ISBN 978-1407-18320-6

Printed and bound by Bell and Bain Ltd, Glasgow
Papers used by Scholastic Limited are made from wood grown in sustainable forests.

Acknowledgements
The publishers gratefully acknowledge permission to reproduce the following copyright material: **Bloodaxe Books** for 'Letters from Yorkshire' by Maura Dooley from *Sound Barrier Poems: 1982–2002* by Maura Dooley, (Bloodaxe Books, 2002); **David Higham Associates** for 'Eden Rock' by Charles Causley from *Collected Poems 1951–2000* by Charles Causley, (Picador, 2000); **Faber & Faber** for 'Mother, any distance' by Simon Armitage from *Book of Matches* by Simon Armitage, (Faber & Faber, 2001) and for 'Follower' by Seamus Heaney from *Opened Ground* by Seamus Heaney, (Faber & Faber, 2001); **Rogers, Coleridge & White** for 'Before You Were Mine' by Carol Ann Duffy from *Mean Time* by Carol Ann Duffy, (Picador, 2013) and for 'Winter Swans' by Owen Sheers from *SKIRRID HILL* by Owen Sheers, (Seren, 2005); **The Peters Fraser and Dunlop Group** on behalf of the Estate of Cecil Day-Lewis for 'Walking Away' by Cecil Day-Lewis from *The Gate and Other Poems* by Cecil Day-Lewis, (Cape, 1962); **The Rialto** for 'Climbing My Grandfather' by Andrew Waterhouse from *In* by Andrew Waterhouse, (The Rialto, 2000); **Guardian News & Media Ltd** for quotation from 'Why my father Cecil Day-Lewis's poem Walking Away stands the test of time' letter by Sean Day-Lewis, (*The Guardian*, 2018) and for quotation from 'Andrew Waterhouse Poet who unravelled life's paradoxes with a vivid and uncluttered imagination' obituary by Sean O'Brien, (*The Guardian*, 2001); **Lidia Vianu** for quotation from 'Interview with Maura Dooley' essay-interview by Lidia Vianu, (*Desperado Essay-Interviews*, 2009)

Every effort has been made to trace copyright holders for the works reproduced in this book, and the publishers apologise for any inadvertent omissions.

Note from the publisher:
Please use this product in conjunction with the official specification and sample assessment materials. Ask your teacher if you are unsure where to find them.

Contents

Check your answers on the free revision app or at www.scholastic.co.uk/gcse

How to use this book

This Study Guide is designed to help you prepare effectively for your AQA GCSE English literature exam question on Poetry anthology – Cluster 1: Love and relationships (Paper 2, Section B).

The content has been organised to allow you to work through the whole of cluster 1 step by step, one poem at a time. You can choose the order in which you would like to study the poems. However, you should ensure that you work through *all* of the content in the book. This will build confidence and deepen your knowledge and understanding of all the poems.

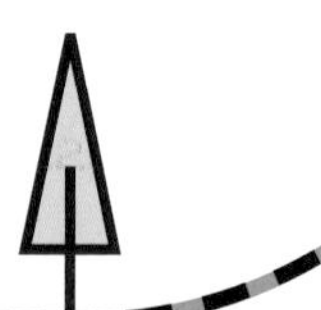

Know the poems

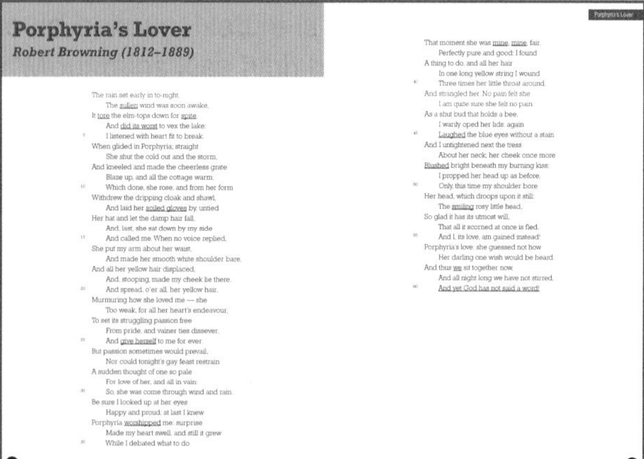

1 It is very important that you know the poems well. Read and study them. Make up your own mind about them. The poems in this Study Guide are set out on the page with every five lines marked for ease of reference. Some words and phrases are underlined for analysis within the guide. Add your own annotations to the poem, exploring more of its details and their effects. Choose details for yourself but do also include the underlined words or phrases. You might like to do your annotations after you have read the full analysis of each poem as outlined in step 2.

Cluster 1: Love and relationships

2 The **Cluster 1: Love and relationships section** on pages 10–75 takes you through the anthology poems one at a time. They provide analysis of themes, contexts, language, structure and form of every poem.

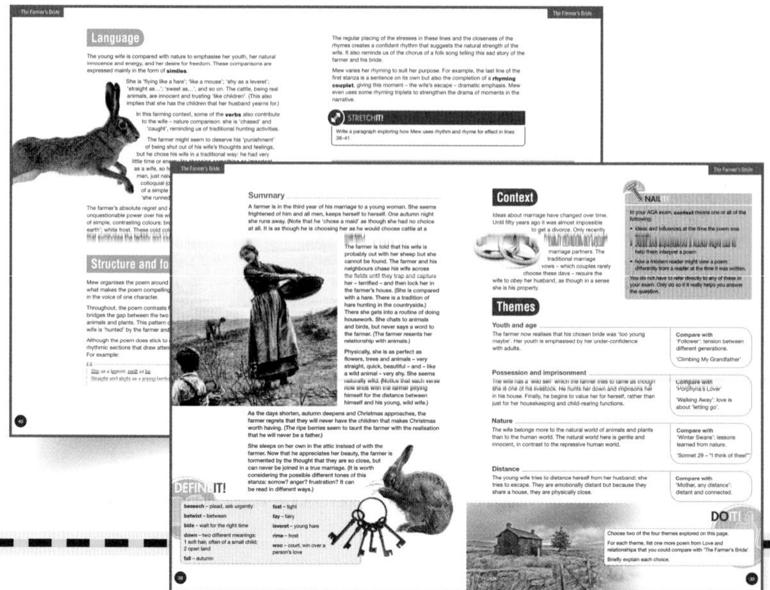

Essentials

3 At the end of the poems section, you will find essential information on pages 76 and 77 which focuses on the overarching themes and sub-themes in the Cluster.

This section will help you understand how to write a good answer to the question in Section B. Additional activities are provided for you to work through and practise.

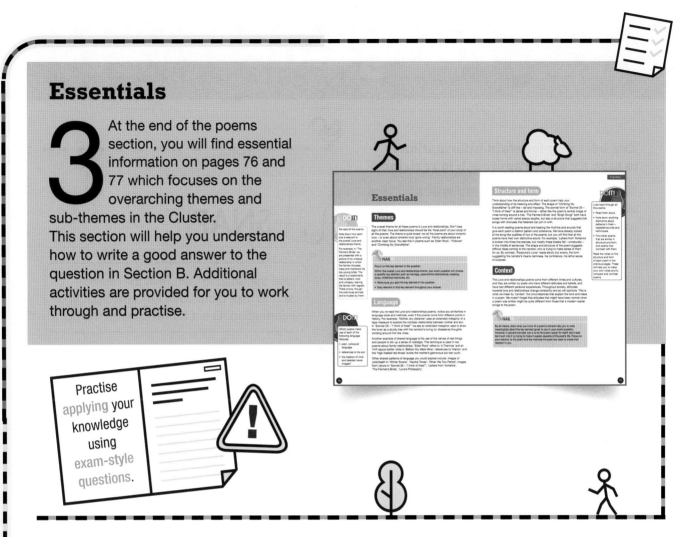

Practise applying your knowledge using exam-style questions.

Doing well in your AQA exam

4 Finally, you will find an extended 'Doing well in your AQA exam' section which guides you through the process of understanding questions, and planning and writing answers.

Stick to the TIME LIMITS you will need to in the exam.

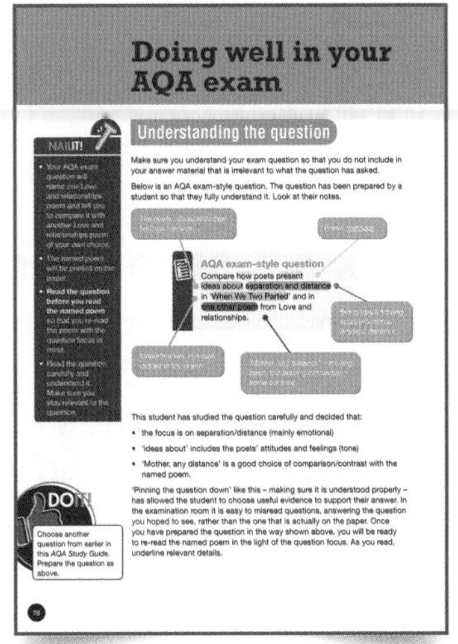

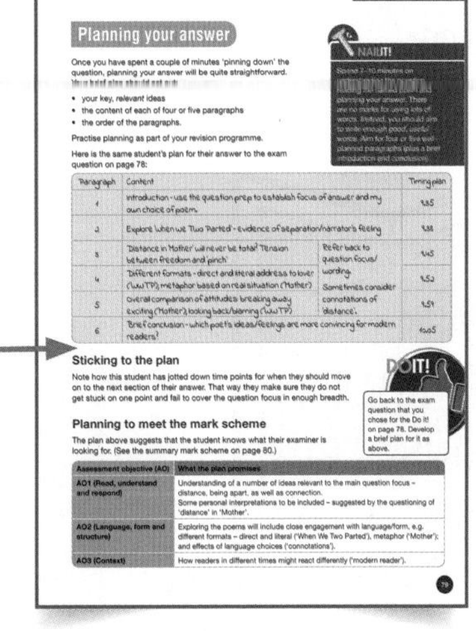

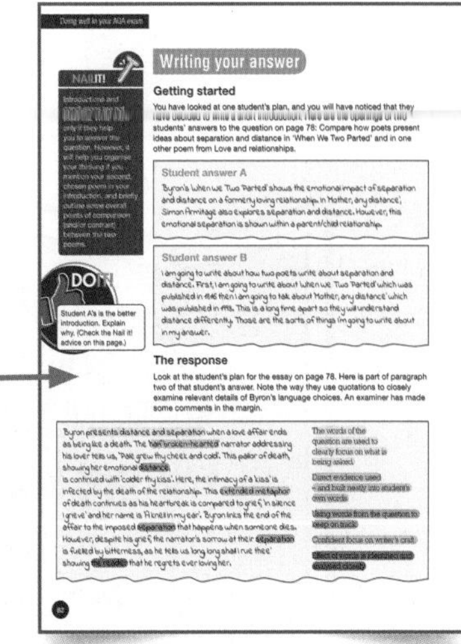

Features of this guide

The best way to retain information is to take an active approach to revision.

Throughout this book, you will find lots of features that will make your revision an active, successful process.

SNAP IT!

Use the Snap it! feature in the revision app to take pictures of key concepts and information. Great for revision on the go!

DEFINE IT!

Explains the meaning of difficult words from the poems.

Callouts Additional explanations of important points.

words shown in **purple bold** can be found in the glossary on pages 86–87

Find methods of relaxation that work for you throughout the revision period.

Regular exercise helps stimulate the brain and will help you relax.

DO IT!

Activities to embed your knowledge and understanding and prepare you for the exam.

NAIL IT!

Succinct and vital tips on how to do well in your exam.

STRETCH IT!

Provides content that stretches you further.

REVIEW IT!

Helps you to consolidate and understand what you have learned before moving on.

Revise in pairs or small groups and deliver presentations on topics to each other.

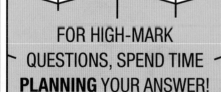

FOR HIGH-MARK QUESTIONS, SPEND TIME PLANNING YOUR ANSWER!

AQA exam-style question

AQA exam-style sample questions based on the poem shown are given on some pages. Use the sample mark scheme on page 80 to help you assess your responses. This will also help you understand what you could do to improve your response.

FREE REVISION APP

- The **free revision app** can be downloaded to your mobile phone (iOS and Android), making **on-the go-revision** easy.
- Use the revision calendar to help map out your revision in the lead-up to the exam.
- Complete multiple-choice questions and create your own **SNAPIT!** revision cards.

www.scholastic.co.uk/gcse

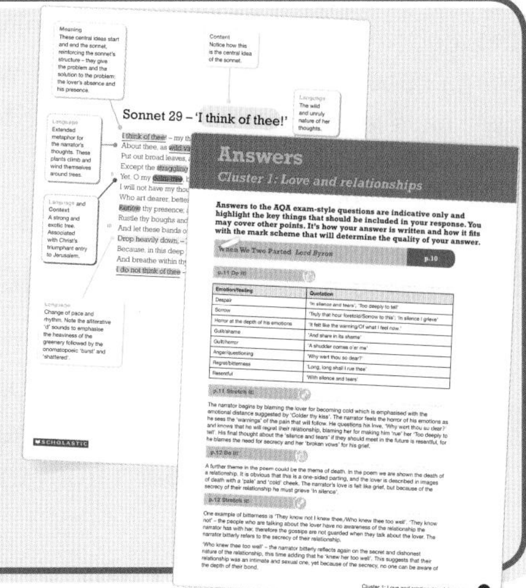

Online answers and additional resources

All of the tasks in this book are designed to get you thinking and to consolidate your understanding through thought and application. Therefore, it is important to write your own answers before checking. Use a separate piece of paper so that you can draft your response and work out the best way of answering.

Online you will find a copy of each poem with detailed annotations. Do not look at those until you have explored the poem thoroughly for yourself.

Get plenty of sleep, especially the night before an exam.

LOOK AFTER YOURSELF

Help your brain by looking after your whole body!

Once you have worked through a section, you can check your answers to Do it!, Stretch it!, Review it! and the exam practice sections on the app or at **www.scholastic.co.uk/gcse**. Annotated poems are available at **www.scholastic.co.uk/gcse-poetry**.

An introduction to your AQA poetry anthology – Cluster 1

NAIL IT!

- Keep a close watch on the time in your exam. Don't spend more than 45 minutes on the modern prose or drama question or you will have less time to write your answer to the Love and relationships question in Section B (40 minutes) or the unseen question in Section C (50 minutes).

Why study Love and relationships poetry?

Even before you read your collection of poetry, you will have considered the nature of love and its impact on our lives. Love is not a modern invention, it has been written about, depicted through art and sung about throughout our history. This cluster of poems, Love and relationships, gives us an overview of how poets have viewed our loving relationships from 1816 to the present day. However, this love isn't all hearts and flowers and romantic love. We are shown family ties and the need to break away from those ties; we are shown the pain of watching a child grow into adulthood and what happens when love dies and bitterness sets in.

What is the aim of the Love and relationships collection?

The aim of the collection is to show us the many forms of love that unify us across history. If we wish to grow as people who can experience all the joys and trials that love can bring, through a whole range of relationships, we can learn from the varied experiences these poets bring us.

Love and relationships poetry in your AQA exam

Love and relationships is examined in Section B (the second section) of the second AQA GCSE English Literature exam, Paper 2 Modern Texts and Poetry. Here is how it fits into the overall assessment framework:

Paper 1 Time: **1 hour 45 minutes**	**Paper 2** Time: **2 hours 15 minutes**
Section A: Shakespeare	Section A: Modern prose or drama
Section B: 19th-century novel	**Section B: Poetry anthology Cluster 1: Love and relationships**
	Section C: Unseen poetry

There will be just one question on the Love and relationships cluster and you should not answer the question on the other cluster (i.e. Power and conflict). Only answer the Love and relationships question. You should spend **40 minutes** planning and writing your answer to the question. There are 30 marks available for this question.

Your Love and relationships question will come with a copy of the selected poem from the cluster printed on your exam paper. You will find the question just before the poem. The question will ask you to compare a theme from the given poem with one other poem of your choice from the Love and relationships cluster. You must answer the question in relation to the printed poem and to one other poem that you have chosen for yourself.

Poems organised by theme

Secrecy
Porphyria's Lover
Singh Song!
When We Two Parted

Admiration/ worship/ possession
Before You Were Mine
Climbing My Grandfather
Follower
Letters from Yorkshire
Love's Philosophy
Porphyria's Lover
Sonnet 29 – 'I think of thee!'
Singh Song!

Separation/ absence/distance
Eden Rock
Letters from Yorkshire
Love's Philosophy
Mother, any distance
Neutral Tones
Sonnet 29 – 'I think of thee!'
The Farmer's Bride
Walking Away
When We Two Parted
Winter Swans

Family ties
Climbing My Grandfather
Eden Rock
Follower
Before You Were Mine
Mother, any distance
Walking Away

Marriage and relationships (positive and negative)
Winter Swans
Singh Song!
The Farmer's Bride
Porphyria's Lover
Sonnet 29 – 'I think of thee!'
Neutral Tones

Breaking away
Follower
Mother, any distance
Walking Away
When We Two Parted

Childhood memories
Eden Rock
Follower
Mother, any distance
Walking Away
Before You Were Mine
Climbing My Grandfather

Romantic love
Love's Philosophy
Porphyria's Lover
Singh Song!
Sonnet 29 – 'I Think of Thee!'
When We Two Parted

Nature
Letters from Yorkshire
Porphyria's Lover
Sonnet 29 – 'I think of thee!'
The Farmer's Bride
Winter Swans

Love lost/ heartbreak
Neutral Tones
The Farmer's Bride
Winter Swans
When We Two Parted

Parent/child
Before You Were Mine
Mother, any distance
Eden Rock
Follower

DO IT!

For each theme, choose two poems that are relevant to the theme but have contrasting points of view. For example:

'Sonnet 29 - "I think of thee!"' and 'Porphyria's Lover'. In both poems, we see obsessive love. This love is positive, resulting in a fulfilled relationship in 'Sonnet 29 - "I think of thee!"' and a dark view of a relationship in 'Porphyria's Lover' with the man murdering his love.

When We Two Parted

Lord Byron (1788–1824)

When we two parted
In silence and tears,
Half broken-hearted
To sever for years,
Pale grew thy cheek and cold,
Colder thy kiss;
Truly that hour foretold
Sorrow to this.

The dew of the morning
Sunk chill on my brow –
It felt like the warning
Of what I feel now.
Thy vows are all broken,
And light is thy fame;
I hear thy name spoken,
And share in its shame.

They name thee before me,
A knell in mine ear;
A shudder comes o'er me –
Why wert thou so dear?
They know not I knew thee,
Who knew thee too well –
Long, long shall I rue thee,
Too deeply to tell.

In secret we met –
In silence I grieve,
That thy heart could forget,
Thy spirit deceive.
If I should meet thee
After long years,
How should I greet thee? –
With silence and tears.

Summary

In this poem, a **narrator** regrets the end of a deep and secret relationship. The narrator remembers when he and his lover separated. They parted 'in silence and tears' when the lover became cold to him, and he still feels that sorrow.

He confirms this idea of continuing sadness at the start of the second **stanza**. He accuses his lover of breaking promises to him, thus damaging her own reputation and bringing shame on them both.

People mention the lover by name to the narrator. Hearing the lover's name causes the narrator pain, and he wonders why the lover was ever so special to him. The narrator reveals that the gossips do not know of his close relationship with the lover, a relationship he now deeply regrets and is unable to talk about.

He recalls that they met secretly, therefore he has to grieve in silence over how easily the lover seems to have forgotten the relationship and their promises. The narrator predicts that if he meets his lover again after many years, he still won't be able to express his feelings or make accusations, but will still be tearful.

(Note that the gender of the narrator and the lover are not mentioned in the poem. We have used 'he' here but there is nothing in the poem to suggest that the narrator is a man.)

STRETCH IT!

What evidence is there that the narrator blames the lover?

DEFINE IT!

brow – forehead

fame – reputation

foretold – predicted

knell – sound of a funeral bell

light – not heavy

o'er – over

rue – regret

sever – cut

thou/thee/thy – you/your

vows – promises

wert – were

DO IT!

List the narrator's feelings about the ending of the relationship. Find a quotation to support each feeling, for example, despair – 'In silence and tears'; guilt and shame – 'And share in its shame'.

Context

Byron was well known in his society as a notorious womaniser. His reputation was that he left a string of broken hearts behind him. However, in this poem Byron's narrator is suffering the pain of heartbreak and expects to be broken hearted for years in the future. It can be misleading to guess that Byron is writing from personal experience. The important question to ask ourselves is whether Byron effectively evokes the bitterness and pain surrounding heartbreak. If we feel that he does this, how did this man described as 'mad, bad and dangerous to know' by Lady Caroline Lamb manage to sum up these feelings so effectively?

Themes

Love

Byron shows the reader what happens when love grows cold and a relationship ends. The title describes this parting factually and unemotionally which does not represent the heartbreak the reader sees throughout the poem. The narrator can only listen as 'They name thee before me' and can only respond to his heartbreak with 'silence and tears'.

Compare with
'Neutral Tones': this poem also explores the end of a relationship.

Sorrow

From the very first stanza we see 'tears', heartbreak and 'sorrow'. This sorrow moves to bitterness as the narrator questions 'Why wert thou so dear?', suggesting that he will 'long, long' regret ('rue') their relationship. However, this regret is too deeply felt to 'tell'.

Compare with
'Walking Away': here sorrow/loss is shown through parental love.

Promises and fidelity

Here we see what happens in a relationship when promises and 'vows are all broken'. The central relationship in the poem was a 'secret' relationship. All 'warning' signs of the lover's growing distance were missed as the cold 'kiss' should have 'foretold' the narrator's later 'sorrow'.

Compare with
'Singh Song!': in this poem, secrecy occurs within a marriage rather than within an illicit relationship.

DO IT!

What other themes can you find in the poem? Briefly explain one additional theme.

Time

The narrator examines how time will not heal his pain. He reflects on a break-up that happened 'years' before, but he knows that the pain will be just as intense in the future. The poem comes full circle as the 'silence and tears' will not end with the passing of time.

Compare with
'Winter Swans': the lovers' distance at the start of the poem is healed by the end. Silence is used to show distance.

STRETCH IT!

Choose one quotation to show the narrator's bitterness and write up to 100 words explaining the meaning and effect of that example.

Language

Throughout the poem, Byron uses images of cold, silence and death to show the end of the relationship that the narrator will 'grieve' in 'silence'. As the lover becomes distant her cheek becomes 'cold', like in death, but the kiss is 'colder'. The narrator's tone is sad, but clearly they blame the lover for being unfaithful, distant and dishonest. This mixed tone of grief and accusation runs throughout.

The voice of the poem is conversational which is helped by the use of short lines. The **effect** of this conversational tone suggests that the narrator is thinking things through in an almost natural way.

Structure and form

The poem is written in four eight-line stanzas with a regular **rhyme** scheme. This regular **structure** and rhyme scheme suggest that the narrator/poet can control this element unlike his regret and heartbreak. The structure is circular with the narrator beginning and ending the poem with 'silence and tears', suggesting that this heartbreak is never-ending.

The **rhythm** of the poem is fairly regular with two **stressed** syllables in each line. For example:

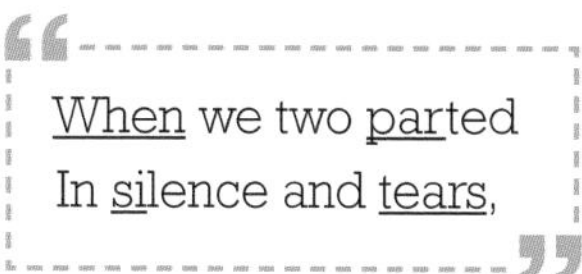

> When we two parted
> In silence and tears,

This pattern continues until we reach the line:

> Pale grew thy cheek and cold,

This change in rhythm is more like natural speech. Here Byron is describing a terrible change in the relationship, an event that is so great it is like a death. The change in rhythm highlights this development.

REVIEW IT!

1 What do we learn from the word 'sever'?
2 What does 'Colder thy kiss' suggest about their relationship?
3 What happens to the lovers' vows?
4 How does the narrator react when the lover's name is mentioned?
5 What does the word 'knell' mean as it is used in the poem?
6 What is the poem's rhyme scheme?
7 What could be the message of the poem?
8 Sum up the tone of the poem.
9 What does the narrator mean by calling the lover's reputation 'light'?
10 What could the narrator mean by 'I hear thy name spoken,/And share in its shame'?

AQA exam-style question

Compare how poets present heartbreak in 'When We Two Parted' and in one other poem from Love and relationships.

[30 marks]

DO IT!

- Add your own annotations to the poem, exploring more of its details and their effects. Include the underlined words or phrases.
- Online you will find a copy of the poem with more detailed annotations.

Love's Philosophy

Percy Bysshe Shelley (1792–1822)

The fountains mingle with the river
And the rivers with the Ocean,
The winds of Heaven mix for ever
With a sweet emotion;
Nothing in the world is single;
All things by a law divine
in one another's being mingle –
Why not I with thine?

See the mountains kiss high Heaven
And the waves clasp one another;
No sister-flower would be forgiven
If it disdain'd its brother:
And the sunlight clasps the earth,
And the moonbeams kiss the sea –
what are all these kissings worth,
If thou kiss not me?

Summary

The narrator is putting forward his logical argument as to why his lover should be together with him and kiss him. The poem is written as if it is one person speaking and each stanza ends with a question. We do not hear the response to either of these questions. (Note that the gender of the narrator and the lover are not mentioned in the poem. We have used 'he' here but there is nothing in the poem to suggest that the narrator is a man.)

In the first stanza, the narrator lists elements of the natural world that may seem to be on their own, but in fact, are joined together. The 'fountains mingle with the river' then those 'rivers' mix with the 'Ocean'. The stanza ends with the question: if nothing in the world is solitary, then why can't we share this togetherness? (Note the way the narrator uses these images from nature to show that togetherness is natural.)

The second stanza brings in the idea that all things within the natural world kiss and embrace. The 'mountains kiss high Heaven' and the 'waves clasp one another'. Even flowers are not alone and cannot be lonely if they are surrounded by other flowers. The narrator completes his argument with the idea that if all of these elements are together and kiss, then he and his lover should kiss too. (Note the use of sensuous images throughout the poem – 'mingle', 'clasp' – that end in 'kiss'.)

DEFINE IT!

clasp – to grip or grasp

disdain'd – to look down on, to sneer at

fountain – a spring

law divine – God's law

mingle – mix together

philosophy – the study of knowledge, reality and existence

sweet – pleasurable

DO IT!

Where do you think this conversation takes place? In a room? Within the natural world? Explain your ideas.

Context

Shelley's poetry and prose use images and make connections to the natural world. Here he uses these connections to build a persuasive argument. Often in his poetry he shows nature as a force that is untamed and more powerful than humankind. Here we see him using nature as a guiding force to show his lover how to act.

NAIL IT!

Examiners say that biographical or historical details that are not relevant to the question do not support students' responses in the examination (for example, 'Shelley was born in Sussex'). Remember that your interpretation of the poem and your response to the question should be the focus of your answer.

Themes

Love

In this poem, love is unrequited; a one-sided love. Shelley's narrator has to work hard to build his carefully reasoned argument to persuade his love that they should be together and kiss.

Compare with
'When We Two Parted': this poem explores a one-sided love.

Connections and unions

The key message of the poem is that everything within nature is part of a pair and this union – physical love – is natural and normal. Even irrational 'Love' is paired with rational 'Philosophy' in the poem's title. These ideas are presented as 'facts' – assertions – to build his argument.

Compare with
'Mother, any distance': the connection between the mother and son is shown through the image of a 'spool of tape'.

Nature and the natural world

The natural world is used as a model of how the lovers should behave. Nature is personified as enjoying connections as 'Mountains kiss high heaven' and 'sunlight clasps the earth'.

Compare with
'Sonnet 29 – "I think of thee!"': thoughts about the lover are expressed in natural images.

Disappointment

The narrator's playful argument is built through a series of natural images. However, we do not hear the response to the two questions posed in the poem. Desperation creeps in as the narrator even refers to divine law, 'All things by a law divine/… mingle', suggesting that these connections are God's law.

Compare with
'The Farmer's Bride': he traps his young wife, but cannot gain her love.

What clues can you find in the poem that this is a conversation that has happened before?

STRETCHIT!

Look at the title of the poem and write up to 100 words explaining its meaning and effect.

Language

Throughout the poem, Shelley/the narrator uses sensuous images pointing out to his lover this is happening in the natural world, so they should act like this too. Waters 'mingle', winds 'mix', mountains 'kiss', waves 'clasp' – this **language** of touch is also the language of intimacy.

The tone of the poem is playful, with the narrator's list-like examples from the natural world building a logical argument. This suggests that the narrator is pointing out details within the landscape, conversationally, to persuade his lover to his point of view. Notice how the dash at the end of line 14 breaks this tone as he demands finally, 'what are all those kissings worth,/If thou kiss not me?'.

Structure and form

The ideas in the poem are organised into two eight–line stanzas with repeated ideas and images and tight ABABCDCD rhyme-scheme. Each idea shows how a natural form ('mountains', 'rivers', 'flowers') does not exist alone, building a reasoned argument showing how the narrator wishes his lover to follow nature's example. The structure is based on an argument – an elaborated point of view – to persuade the lover. The reader does not hear the lover's response.

Shelley uses **anaphora** to build his argument. This also reflects the language and rhythms of biblical psalms, linking to 'law divine'. The repeated structure 'And the waves… And the sunlight…' builds during the second stanza to climax with the dramatic 'what are all these kissings worth/If thou kiss not me?' (He suggests that if this is true within nature then this must also be true of the lovers.)

In many of the poem's lines, Shelley uses **trochaic metre** (alternating between stressed and unstressed syllables). The stress is on the first syllable, 'See the mountains kiss high Heaven' which can create a sad or menacing mood. (Trochaic metre is often used in poetry about war or death.) However, trochaic metre is also used in magical incantations (think of Shakespeare's witches). Maybe the narrator is seeking to cast his spell over his lover?

1 In stanza one, what is the key idea?
2 In stanza two, what is the key idea?
3 What does Shelley mean by 'sweet' in this poem?
4 Why do you think Shelley introduces God's law, 'law divine', to his argument?
5 Other than 'law divine', find one other religious reference in the poem.
6 Find two images of sensual or physical intimacy.
7 Describe the poem's rhyme scheme.
8 What is the effect of the dash (–) used at the end of line 14?
9 What do you understand by: 'No sister-flower would be forgiven/If it disdain'd its brother'?
10 What does Shelley suggest nature can teach us about love? Explain your ideas.

- Add your own annotations to the poem, exploring more of its details and their effects. Include the underlined words or phrases.
- Online you will find a copy of the poem with more detailed annotations.

AQA exam-style question

Compare how poets present rejection in 'Love's Philosophy' and in one other poem from Love and relationships.

[30 marks]

Porphyria's Lover
Robert Browning (1812–1889)

The rain set early in to-night,
The <u>sullen</u> wind was soon awake,
It <u>tore</u> the elm-tops down for <u>spite</u>,
And <u>did its worst</u> to vex the lake:
I listened with heart fit to break.
When glided in Porphyria; straight
She shut the cold out and the storm,
And kneeled and made the cheerless grate
Blaze up, and all the cottage warm;
Which done, she rose, and from her form
Withdrew the dripping cloak and shawl,
And laid her <u>soiled gloves</u> by, untied
Her hat and let the damp hair fall,
And, last, she sat down by my side
And called me. When no voice replied,
She put my arm about her waist,
And made her smooth white shoulder bare,
And all her yellow hair displaced,
And, stooping, made my cheek lie there,
And spread, o'er all, her yellow hair,
Murmuring how she loved me – she
Too weak, for all her heart's endeavour,
To set its struggling passion free
From pride, and vainer ties dissever,
And <u>give herself</u> to me for ever.
But passion sometimes would prevail,
Nor could tonight's gay feast restrain
A sudden thought of one so pale
For love of her, and all in vain:
So, she was come through wind and rain.
Be sure I looked up at her eyes
Happy and proud; at last I knew
Porphyria <u>worshipped</u> me: surprise
Made my heart swell, and still it grew
While I debated what to do.

That moment she was mine, mine, fair,
Perfectly pure and good: I found
A thing to do, and all her hair
In one long yellow string I wound
Three times her little throat around,
And strangled her. No pain felt she;
I am quite sure she felt no pain.
As a shut bud that holds a bee,
I warily oped her lids: again
Laughed the blue eyes without a stain.
And I untightened next the tress
About her neck; her cheek once more
Blushed bright beneath my burning kiss:
I propped her head up as before,
Only, this time my shoulder bore
Her head, which droops upon it still:
The smiling rosy little head,
So glad it has its utmost will,
That all it scorned at once is fled,
And I, its love, am gained instead!
Porphyria's love: she guessed not how
Her darling one wish would be heard.
And thus we sit together now,
And all night long we have not stirred,
And yet God has not said a word!

Summary

Porphyria's lover – the narrator of the poem – is alone in his cottage, heartbroken to think that Porphyria will not brave the storm outside to come and visit him.

Suddenly, she arrives. She stokes the fire, removes her wet clothing and sits next to the narrator. She calls his name, puts his arm round her and rests his head on her bare shoulder, before covering his face in her long yellow hair. She quietly says, 'I love you'. (We only have the narrator's word for all this. Perhaps he is describing what he wants rather than what actually happens.)

The narrator tells us that the only thing that stops Porphyria from giving herself to him 'for ever' are the ties she has to ordinary conventions and her sense of duty to others. Tonight her passion for the narrator has given her the strength to break those ties, brave the storm and come to visit him. (The narrator always presents himself in a theatrically pathetic way: he has been neglected by Porphyria who lacks the moral courage to 'do the right thing'.)

When he looks in her eyes he sees that she 'worships' him. This surprises him but makes him proud. He wonders how he can make this moment – when she is 'perfectly pure and good' – last forever.

He strangles her with her own hair, assuring himself that she felt no pain. He opens her eyes 'warily', undoes the noose of her hair and kisses her reddening cheek. Then he rests her head on his shoulder. (This is a shock because the killing of Porphyria is so sudden and so calmly carried out.)

They sit like that all night, with the narrator thinking about how Porphyria has now got what she always wanted – happiness and him forever. He notices that God is silent about what he has done.

DEFINE IT!

dissever – break

elm tops – the tops of elm trees

endeavour – try

fair – beautiful

gay – lively and happy

grate – fireplace

oped – opened

straight – straight away

sullen – sulky

tress – lock of hair

vainer – prouder (but in a selfish way)

vex – annoy, unsettle

warily – cautiously

Context

Robert Browning was a famous Victorian poet who wrote a number of dramatic **monologues**, such as 'Porphyria's Lover'. It is important to note that in a dramatic monologue it is the narrator's view, not the poet's, that is being expressed. Browning expressed views in favour of women's equality and against slavery.

Readers will probably doubt that the narrator really does love Porphyria: who would kill someone they genuinely loved? The narrator's actions might seem more motivated by madness and delusion than by love.

Themes

Secrecy

It is likely that the narrator's relationship with Porphyria is secret. The storm acts as a cover for her escape. The image of the 'soiled gloves' she takes off hints that their relationship is forbidden or 'dirty' (disapproved of) in some sense.

Compare with
'When We Two Parted': 'They know not I knew thee.'

'Singh Song!': the lovers keep the depth of their passion secret.

Loyalty and honesty

The narrator presents himself as a helpless victim of Porphyria's neglect: she is to blame because she lacks the courage to be loyal to him and her passion, rather than to respectability and social appearances ('vainer ties').

Compare with
'When We Two Parted': the narrator blames his/her lover for their parting.

Possession

The narrator wants to possess Porphyria, to control her completely. When he feels sure she loves him, he decides to kill her so that she will be 'mine, mine' forever. He imagines her 'utmost will' to be to 'give herself' to him.

Compare with
'Before You Were Mine'

'The Farmer's Bride': he traps his young wife, but cannot gain her love.

Nature

Here nature – in the shape of a storm – is a threat to their relationship, but is a protection to Porphyria. It perhaps emphasises that their relationship is 'not meant to be'.

Compare with
'Sonnet 29 – "I think of thee!"': trees are used as an **extended metaphor**.

'Letters from Yorkshire'

DO IT!

Choose two of the four themes explored on this page. For each theme, list one more poem that you could compare with 'Porphyria's Lover'. Briefly explain each choice.

Language

Although the poem includes some archaic words (words we no longer use) such as 'dissever' and 'oped', what is striking about it is its use of ordinary, often very short words. Here is what one student wrote about this:

Browning gives the narrator very ordinary, non-poetic language to speak to us. For example, her throat is 'little', not 'delicate'. This colloquial language makes him sound ordinary and believable, and that ordinariness makes him even more frightening.

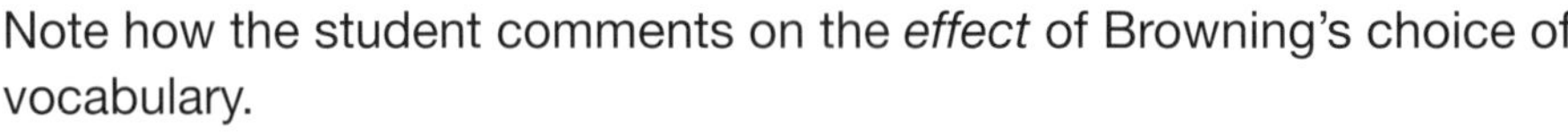

Note how the student comments on the *effect* of Browning's choice of vocabulary.

The images Browning creates are often very striking. His **personification** of the storm as something 'spiteful' supports the narrator's presentation of himself as a victim rather than a murderer. The image of the narrator giving the dead Porphyria a 'burning kiss' is shocking enough, but the kiss also 'burns' as though it is full of passion or perhaps punishment.

STRETCHIT!

Choose one other example of ordinary language in the poem and write up to 100 words explaining the meaning and effect of that example.

Structure and form

The poem is a dramatic monologue given by a single narrator. The effect of this is that we only get the narrator's point of view, and because this narrator seems insane, his version of events is 'unreliable' – we cannot trust it to be accurate. That is stimulating for the reader: we have to try to deduce Porphyria's true feelings and motives.

The poem is organised into a series of five-line groups. In each group of five, lines one and three rhyme, and so do lines two, four and five. For example:

> …Withdrew the dripping cloak and shawl,
> And laid her soiled gloves by, untied
> Her hat and let the damp hair fall,
> And, last, she sat down by my side
> And called me. When no voice replied,…

However, these five-line groups are not always self-contained units of meaning. The sense of the above example runs on from the previous group and runs into the next one. The poem's most important divisions are dramatic sections and turning points, and – roughly speaking – these are marked by full stops.

The poem has a regular rhyme scheme and its lines are **iambic tetrameters**. That means they have (mostly) eight syllables and four stresses, alternating between unstressed and stressed syllables. For example:

And all night long we have not stirred

Because **iambic** lines stress the final syllable, any rhymes are strengthened.

Effects

Browning uses the poem's patterns – the rhyme scheme, the iambic tetrameters and the five-line groupings – to lead the reader through what is quite a long poem that is not divided into verses. On the other hand, he uses other methods to slow the poem down and make it sound more like a real person thinking aloud. These methods include plain language, breaks in the middle of lines, and stretching the sense of some lines on to the next line (**enjambment**).

1 In the poem, what does the word 'vex' mean?
2 Where has Porphyria been when she visits the narrator?
3 How does the narrator kill Porphyria?
4 What are the first three things the narrator does after killing Porphyria?
5 Which words and phrases suggest that the narrator sees Porphyria as his possession and/or his inferior?
6 How many syllables are in an iambic tetrameter, and how many of the syllables are stressed when read aloud?
7 How does the narrator present himself as a victim?
8 How does the narrator know that Porphyria has got 'her darling one wish'?
9 Why could the narrator be considered 'unreliable'?
10 What might Browning be suggesting by the poem's last line? Briefly explain your thoughts.

- Add your own annotations to the poem, exploring more of its details and their effects. Include the highlighted words or phrases.
- Online you will find a copy of the poem with more detailed annotations.

AQA exam-style question

Compare how poets present possessive feelings in 'Porphyria's Lover' and in one other poem from Love and relationships.

[30 marks]

Sonnet 29 – 'I think of thee!'

Elizabeth Barrett Browning (1806–1861)

I think of thee! – my thoughts do twine and bud
About thee, as wild vines, about a tree,
Put out broad leaves, and soon there's nought to see
Except the straggling green which hides the wood.
Yet, O my palm-tree, be it understood
I will not have my thoughts instead of thee
Who art dearer, better! Rather, instantly
Renew thy presence; as a strong tree should,
Rustle thy boughs and set thy trunk all bare,
And let these bands of greenery which insphere thee
Drop heavily down, – burst, shattered, everywhere!
Because, in this deep joy to see and hear thee
And breathe within thy shadow a new air,
I do not think of thee – I am too near thee.

Summary

The narrator speaks directly to her lover. She tells him that she is thinking of him and her thoughts wind around him like vines wrap around a tree until it is hidden by these thoughts 'nought to see'. These thoughts are wild and uncontrolled 'straggling'. (Note the extended metaphor of the tree representing her lover and the vine representing the narrator's thoughts.)

However, she is clear that she would rather have him in person than the idealised vision of him. Her lover is 'better' than any thoughts she could have of him. She demands that he should shake off her thoughts and come to see her, 'Rustle thy boughs'. As he does appear, her thoughts 'burst' and scatter 'everywhere!'. (We need to ask ourselves if he really does appear or does she ask for it to happen.)

The narrator's world is complete with her lover in it. She can experience 'deep joy' and 'breathe...new air'. She is protected and comforted by him: she can 'breathe within thy shadow'. She no longer needs her thoughts of him because she can be with him.

DEFINE IT!

bough – branches of a tree

insphere – to enclose in a sphere

nought – nothing

palm-tree – an exotic tree, strong tree with religious meaning (see 'Language' page 26)

straggling – wild and untended

thee/thy – an archaic, but more intimate form of 'you'/'your'

vines – a climbing plant, for example, grape vine, ivy

STRETCH IT!

Look at this student's view of the narrator's love shown within the sonnet. Do you agree with this viewpoint? Explain your views.

> The type of love within this sonnet is an obsessive form of love. Her thoughts are smothering so much so that her thoughts, described as 'vines', wrap around him until there is 'nought' to see and no image of him remains. This feeling grows like the vines until it 'shattered everywhere', showing the reader how the intensity of her love overwhelms her. Readers may not see this as a healthy form of love.

DO IT!

Explain how the poet uses the extended metaphor of the vine and the tree to show her feelings for her lover.

Context

The poem is part of a sonnet sequence written during Elizabeth Barrett Browning's love affair with Robert Browning. The sonnets were originally intended just for him to read – but after their marriage he persuaded her to publish them. These were written during the Victorian era when love and intimacy, even within a marriage, were not as openly talked about as they are today.

Themes

Love – fulfilment and joy

The tone of the poem is joyous and excited by love. The narrator's thoughts 'twine' about her lover as they develop and 'bud'. This is love that is fulfilled and given back to her by the lover who enables her to 'breathe new air'.

Compare with
'Singh Song!': the joy of love within marriage is explored.

Love – distance

The lover is absent and so at first she can only think of him. She longs for the lover and demands that he comes to her. The narrator wants her lover rather than any idealised version that is created by her thoughts as he is 'dearer, better!'

Compare with
'When We Two Parted': the distance between the lovers is viewed with bitterness.

Nature and the natural world

Thoughts about the lover are expressed in natural images. An extended metaphor of a tree (the lover) and a vine (the narrator) is used to show the relationship. The lover is strong and magnificent. Her love, extensive like the vine leaves, surrounds him.

Compare with
'Love's Philosophy': the natural world is used as a model of how the lovers should behave.

Language

The sonnet uses images from nature to describe the fulfilment of the narrator's love. Her thoughts 'twine' and 'bud' before they 'drop heavily, down' and 'burst'. These are natural, ripe and luscious images. The central extended metaphor shows the lover as a strong and stable tree that she, shown as a vine, surrounds and embraces. This vine can 'put out broad leaves' (her thoughts) until there is 'nought' to see of him, but she understands that it is him she wants rather than any idealised version. The lover is referred to as a 'palm-tree', a tree seen as exotic by the Victorians. It also has religious **connotations** as Christ's followers threw palm leaves at his feet as a sign of their devotion and worship as he entered Jerusalem triumphantly.

The mirroring of 'I think of thee' and 'I do not think of thee' brings the sonnet full circle showing the all-consuming presence of the lover in her thoughts. The echo of 'thee', the intimate form of 'you' which would have been old-fashioned when the poem was written, reinforces this focus.

What do you understand by the lines, 'Renew thy presence; as a strong tree should,/Rustle thy boughs'?

Structure and form

A sonnet is a fourteen-line poem that was often used in love poetry, especially if this love was unrequited. The sonnet form is tightly structured with the first eight lines outlining an issue or problem and the final six lines giving a solution or counter-argument. However, Barrett Browning disrupts this tight structure with a change of direction at line five signalled by the word 'Yet'. Here the structure reflects how Barrett Browning stops the uncontrolled growth of the narrator's thoughts and demands that her lover comes to her ('Renew thy presence'). At this point the iambic **metre** stumbles and breaks down and the rhythm becomes uneven. This emphasises the rush of her thoughts as 'bands of greenery' release him and 'drop heavily down'.

1 What was the usual subject matter for a sonnet?
2 What **metaphor** does the narrator use to describe herself and her lover?
3 Why does the narrator refer to her lover as 'my palm-tree'?
4 Why doesn't the narrator want the vision of her lover created by her thoughts?
5 What does the word 'straggling' suggest about the narrator's thoughts?
6 What is the tone of 'I will not have my thoughts instead of thee'?
7 How do the first and last lines support the structure of this sonnet?
8 Find a quotation to show that the narrator feels safe in her lover's presence.
9 Explain the meaning and effect of the words 'deep joy to see and hear thee'.
10 How do Barrett Browning's word choices help the mood and meaning of the poem? Find and explain two examples.

- Add your own annotations to the poem, exploring more of its details and their effects. Include the highlighted words or phrases.
- Online you will find a copy of the poem with more detailed annotations.

AQA exam-style question

Compare how poets present obsession in 'Sonnet 29 – "I think of thee!"' and in one other poem from Love and relationships.

[30 marks]

Neutral Tones

Thomas Hardy (1840–1928)

We stood by a pond that winter day,
And the sun was white, as though chidden of God,
And a few leaves lay on the starving sod;
  – They had fallen from an ash, and were grey.

Your eyes on me were as eyes that rove
Over tedious riddles of years ago;
And some words played between us to and fro
  On which lost the more by our love.

The smile on your mouth was the deadest thing
Alive enough to have strength to die;
And a grin of bitterness swept thereby
  Like an ominous bird a-wing…

Since then, keen lessons that love deceives,
And wrings with wrong, have shaped to me
Your face, and the God-curst sun, and a tree,
  And a pond edged with greyish leaves.

Summary

The poet recalls a day when he and his partner were standing next to a pond in winter. Leaves from an ash tree lay on the ground. (Notice how the winter scenery seems appropriate for Hardy's gloomy mood.)

Even at that meeting at the pond the poet and his partner are distant from each other and their love seems to have died already: they pick over old disagreements and misunderstandings ('tedious riddles') and they are talking about which of them has been most damaged ('*lost* the more') by their relationship. (Unusually, in this love poem, love is presented as something harmful rather than enriching.)

The only smile on his partner's face was 'the deadest thing' and – just as unpleasant – 'a grin of bitterness'. He remembers this grin now as 'ominous': he should have read it as a sign of the sorrow and misery to come – certainly for him.

Since that day the poet has learned some 'keen' (sharp and bitter) lessons: love deceives and wrongs people. When he recalls his partner's face and the scene that day by the winter pond he is reminded of the lessons he should have learned that day. (Here he is implying, surely, that he is the victim and she is to blame for his sufferings.)

DEFINE IT!

ash – a type of tree

chidden of – told off by

curst – cursed

keen – sharp

rove – wander

sod – soil, earth

tedious – dull, boring

thereby – by there

wring – twist roughly (normally to squeeze out water)

Context

Hardy was a very famous novelist and poet. Gloomy, tragic love was a theme running through much of his writing. He did not always blame women for the failure of love. His most famous novel, *Tess of the D'Urbervilles*, shows men as hypocrites and users of women.

Themes

Lessons learned

The poet has learned that 'love deceives'. However, we could infer that really he means that his partner has deceived him – certainly more than he deceived her.

Compare with:
'When We Two Parted': the idea of 'deception'.

'Walking Away': the poet learns lessons about 'letting go'.

Regrets

The poet regrets that he didn't learn sooner that love is painful and bound to die. The poet understands this lesson through hindsight: he learns it by reimagining a scene that he now understands differently and more fully. It is a very pessimistic poem.

Compare with:
'When We Two Parted': 'long shall I rue thee'

Nature

Here nature mirrors the poet's feelings and their 'dead' relationship: nature too is cold and 'dead' because it is winter. Hardy often used this **pathetic fallacy** technique – choosing an environment that reinforces the mood of the scene he is writing about.

Compare with:
'Eden Rock': it is a 'visit' to nature in the form of a picnic that is the backdrop to Causley's memory.

Language

The poem's use of relatively conversational vocabulary suits the detached, thoughtful mood. Hardy does not want to dramatically condemn love: instead, his quiet language makes it sound like he is pessimistic and accepting. The poem's ending – with its simple list of sights – reinforces this mood of resignation.

The **imagery** links love to death and misery – and the deadness of winter: for example, the earth is 'starving'; her smile is 'the deadest thing', full of 'bitterness'. The fact that her smile is just a 'thing' emphasises the deadness of their relationship. The irony is that her smile is just 'Alive enough to have the strength to die'. This really isn't a *romantic* love poem!

STRETCHIT!

Find Hardy's two references to God.

- Explain what you think he is trying to suggest about God.
- How do these references to God contribute to the poem's mood and meaning?

Structure and form

The poem's coherence comes from the way it is organised. 'Neutral Tones' has:

- consistent imagery linked to death and misery
- a strong mood of defeat and sadness throughout
- an ending that echoes the beginning so as to reinforce the impressions we are given at the start.

The poem is divided into four four-line stanzas. These simple stanzas provide a sort of logical sequence that helps the reader to follow Hardy's point:

1. description of remembered scene
2. the communication between them
3. the signs he should have noted
4. the lessons he has learned.

Although the lines are similar in length, they don't have a regular rhythm: they have different numbers of stresses and these fall at different points. This 'raggedness' supports the quiet thoughtfulness of the poem while the regular rhyme scheme gives back some momentum to the poem's argument: the reader feels as though it is 'going somewhere'.

1. In stanza one, what is the season?
2. In stanza one, what is lying on the ground?
3. What was 'the deadest thing'?
4. Explain in your own words the lesson that the poet says he has learned.
5. What does Hardy's word 'keen' suggest about the lessons?
6. Does the poem have a regular rhythm?
7. Describe the poem's rhyme scheme.
8. What do you understand by 'tedious riddles' in stanza two?
9. How does the poem's title sum up its mood and meaning?
10. How does the poem's language style help the poem's mood and meaning?

- Add your own annotations to the poem, exploring more of its details and their effects. Include the underlined words or phrases.
- Online you will find a copy of the poem with more detailed annotations.

AQA exam-style question

Compare how poets present sadness and disappointment in 'Neutral Tones' and in one other poem from Love and relationships.

[30 marks]

Letters from Yorkshire

Maura Dooley (b.1957)

In February, digging <u>his</u> garden, planting potatoes,
<u>he</u> saw the first lapwings return and came
indoors to write to me, <u>his</u> knuckles singing

as they reddened in the warmth.
<u>It's not romance, simply how things are.</u>
<u>You</u> out there, in the cold, seeing the seasons

turning, me with my heartful of headlines
feeding words onto a blank screen.
Is <u>your</u> life more real because <u>you</u> dig and sow?

<u>You</u> wouldn't say so, breaking ice on a waterbutt,
clearing a path through snow. Still, it's <u>you</u>
who sends me word of that other world

pouring air and light into an envelope. So that
at night, watching the same news in different houses,
our souls tap out messages across the icy miles.

Summary

The title of the poem tells us what it is about – a woman receiving letters from a man in Yorkshire. However, the poem is also about distance, connections and how our lives can be different within the same world.

It is February and the narrator describes the man working in his garden. He sees the lapwings return and goes indoors to write to the narrator. (Notice that this is his first thought when he sees the birds.) The narrator outlines her relationship with the man as we are told that it is 'not romance'. (Notice we are not told what the relationship is – only what it is not. This is the mystery at the heart of the poem.)

The narrator talks of her life which is a life full of 'headlines' and 'feeding words onto a blank screen'. Their different worlds are underlined as she reflects on whether his world is 'more real' because his life is doing physical labour in the natural world. She reflects that he would deny this and he would point out the hardships: 'breaking ice', 'clearing snow'. (There is a sense here that the narrator longs for the world that she hears of as he sends her 'word' of his world.)

Finally, the narrator explores the connection between them as she shows them watching the 'same news' even though they are apart. Despite this distance, their 'souls' connect through messages they 'tap out'. This connection remains despite the miles between them.

DEFINE IT!

lapwings – birds from farmland and wetlands

reddened – made red through warming up after being very cold

waterbutt – a large container for collecting rainwater

DO IT!

Explain what you understand by the line 'It's not romance, simply how things are'.

Context

Maura Dooley is a contemporary British poet. Her poetry often features the themes of love and the natural world using vivid visual images. She likes to explore familiar or commonplace things in her poetry, making them new and unfamiliar.

STRETCH IT!

> "Like many other poets, the 'I' that I use in my poem is sometimes an imagined or borrowed 'I' and not simply me."

Look at the quotation above from an interview with Maura Dooley. How might this help you when reading the poem in Love and relationships?

Themes

Connections

Communication establishes the connection between the narrator and the man. He sees the 'first lapwings' and immediately goes to write the letters in the title. The news in these letters pours 'air and light' – essential elements for growth – into her world. The use of the plural 'Letters' in the title and 'messages' in the final line, suggests that these communications are numerous.

Compare with
'Sonnet 29 – "I think of thee!"': connections, despite absence, within a loving relationship.

Distance

The man is absent and the distance is measured in 'icy miles'. The distance between their worlds is clear as he exists in the natural world where he is 'planting potatoes' – presumably to feed himself whereas she is 'feeding words onto a blank screen'.

Compare with
'When We Two Parted': the distance between the lovers is viewed with bitterness.

Nature and the natural world

The man's life within the natural world is more immediate and vivid, where he carries out physical tasks that enable him to 'see' the lapwings, see the 'seasons/turning' and experience 'his knuckles singing' through cold. She questions whether this is 'more real' than her urban life with her 'heartful of headlines'.

Compare with
'Follower': the narrator watches his father working on the land with admiration.

DO IT!

Find one more theme relevant to 'Letters from Yorkshire' and to Love and relationships.

For the theme, list one more poem that you could compare with 'Letters from Yorkshire'.

Briefly explain your choice.

Language

Dooley uses language from everyday life: 'digging his garden, planting potatoes' – stripped-down, factual accounts of ordinary things. However, the man's life within nature is active: we see him 'digging', he 'saw' the lapwings and 'came/indoors to write' to her. He sees his life as practical, ordinary ('You wouldn't say so, breaking ice on a waterbutt') yet the narrator points out the contrast between them with, 'You out there' while she is 'feeding words onto a blank screen'. The personification of his 'knuckles singing' seems to cause a shift from the distant third person address 'he' to the more intimate, 'you out there'.

In the final stanza, Dooley introduces a mystical, spiritual dimension with the 'air and light' that is poured into the letters as their 'souls tap out messages' suggesting the strength of the connection between them, despite it not being a physical one.

Structure and form

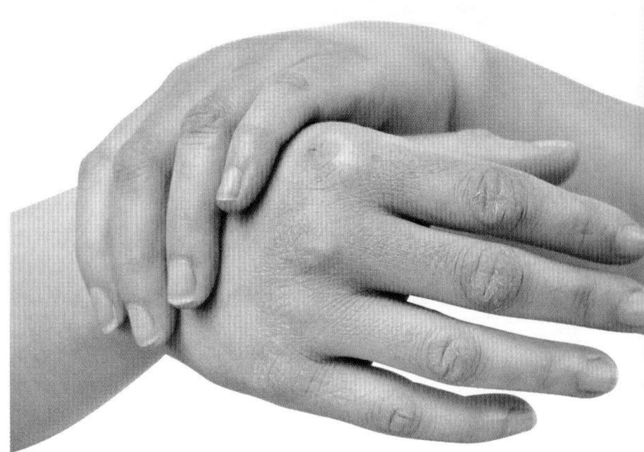

At first glance the structure of the poem is regular, made up of five, unrhymed, three-line stanzas. It is only on closer reading that the flow of ideas between lines and stanzas becomes clear. The description of 'knuckles singing' continues into the second stanza – 'as they reddened' – and this pattern continues with the only exception being the two end-stopped lines in stanzas two and five. Each of these lines provides an important revelation: 'It's not romance, simply how things are', or a realisation about contrasting lives: 'Is your life more real because you dig and sow?'

The structure of the ideas in the poem can be seen as:

- the world the man inhabits
- their relationship
- the world the narrator inhabits
- the nature of their relationship
- their connection.

1 What month is the setting for the poem?
2 Find two quotations that show that it is cold in the garden.
3 When the man sees the lapwings, what does he do?
4 What does 'seeing the seasons/turning' mean?
5 What do you think the narrator does for a job?
6 How does Dooley describe the distance between the man and woman?
7 What does the title of the poem tell us about the communication between the man and the narrator?
8 How does the narrator describe her work in stanza three?
9 How do we know the narrator longs for the man's way of life?
10 Explain your understanding of the relationship between the man and the narrator.

- Add your own annotations to the poem, exploring more of its details and their effects. Include the underlined words or phrases.
- Online you will find a copy of the poem with more detailed annotations.

AQA exam-style question

Compare how poets present rural life in 'Letters from Yorkshire' and in one other poem from Love and relationships.

[30 marks]

The Farmer's Bride

Charlotte Mew (1869–1928)

Three Summers since I chose a maid,
Too young maybe – but more's to do
At harvest-time than bide and woo.
When us was wed she turned afraid
Of love and me and all things human;
Like the shut of a winter's day
Her smile went out, and 'twasn't a woman –
More like a little frightened fay.
One night, in the Fall, she runned away.

'Out 'mong the sheep, her be,' they said,
Should properly have been abed;
But sure enough she wasn't there
Lying awake with her wide brown stare.
So over seven-acre field and up-along across the down
We chased her, flying like a hare
Before our lanterns. To Church-Town
All in a shiver and a scare
We caught her, fetched her home at last
And turned the key upon her, fast.

She does the work about the house
As well as most, but like a mouse:
Happy enough to chat and play
With birds and rabbits and such as they,
So long as men-folk keep away.
'Not near, not near!' her eyes beseech
When one of us comes within reach.
The women say that beasts in stall
Look round like children at her call.
I've hardly heard her speak at all.

Shy as a leveret, swift as he,
Straight and slight as a young larch tree,
Sweet as the first wild violets, she,
To her wild self. But what to me?

The short days shorten and the oaks are brown,
    The blue smoke rises to the low grey sky,
One leaf in the still air falls slowly down,
    A magpie's spotted feathers lie
On the black earth spread white with rime,
The berries redden up to Christmas-time.
    What's Christmas-time without there be
    Some other in the house than we!

    She sleeps up in the attic there
    Alone, poor maid. 'Tis but a stair
Betwixt us. Oh! my God! the down,
The soft young down of her, the brown,
The brown of her – her eyes, her hair, her hair!

Summary

A farmer is in the third year of his marriage to a young woman. She seems frightened of him and all men, keeps herself to herself. One autumn night she runs away. (Note that he 'chose a maid' as though she had no choice at all. It is as though he is choosing her as he would choose cattle at a market.)

The farmer is told that his wife is probably out with her sheep but she cannot be found. The farmer and his neighbours chase his wife across the fields until they trap and capture her – terrified – and then lock her in the farmer's house. (She is compared with a hare. There is a tradition of hare hunting in the countryside.) There she gets into a routine of doing housework. She chats to animals and birds, but never says a word to the farmer. (The farmer resents her relationship with animals.)

Physically, she is as perfect as flowers, trees and animals – very straight, quick, beautiful – and – like a wild animal – very shy. She seems naturally wild. (Notice that each verse now ends with the farmer pitying himself for the distance between himself and his young, wild wife.)

As the days shorten, autumn deepens and Christmas approaches, the farmer regrets that they will never have the children that makes Christmas worth having. (The ripe berries seem to taunt the farmer with the realisation that he will never be a father.)

She sleeps on her own in the attic instead of with the farmer. Now that he appreciates her beauty, the farmer is tormented by the thought that they are so close, but can never be joined in a true marriage. (It is worth considering the possible different tones of this stanza: sorrow? anger? frustration? It can be read in different ways.)

beseech – plead, ask urgently

betwixt – between

bide – wait for the right time

down – two different meanings: 1 soft hair, often of a small child; 2 open land

fall – autumn

fast – tight

fay – fairy

leveret – young hare

rime – frost

woo – court, win over a person's love

Context

Ideas about marriage have changed over time. Until fifty years ago it was almost impossible to get a divorce. Only recently have husbands and wives been considered *equal* marriage partners. The traditional marriage vows – which couples rarely choose these days – require the wife to *obey* her husband, as though in a sense she is his property.

NAIL IT!

In your AQA exam, **context** means one or all of the following:

- ideas and influences at the time the poem was written
- ideas and expectations a reader might use to help them interpret a poem
- how a modern reader might view a poem differently from a reader at the time it was written.

You do not *have* to refer directly to any of these in your exam. Only do so if it really helps you answer the question.

Themes

Youth and age

The farmer now realises that his chosen bride was 'too young maybe'. Her youth is emphasised by her under-confidence with adults.

Compare with
'Follower': tension between different generations.

'Climbing My Grandfather'

Possession and imprisonment

The wife has a 'wild self' which the farmer tries to tame as though she is one of his livestock. He hunts her down and imprisons her in his house. Finally, he begins to value her for herself, rather than just for her housekeeping and child-rearing functions.

Compare with
'Porphyria's Lover'

'Walking Away': love is about 'letting go'.

Nature

The wife belongs more to the natural world of animals and plants than to the human world. The natural world here is gentle and innocent, in contrast to the repressive human world.

Compare with
'Winter Swans': lessons learned from nature.

'Sonnet 29 – "I think of thee!"'

Distance

The young wife tries to distance herself from her husband; she tries to escape. They are emotionally distant but because they share a house, they are physically close.

Compare with
'Mother, any distance': distant and connected.

DO IT!

Choose two of the four themes explored on this page.

For each theme, list one more poem from Love and relationships that you could compare with 'The Farmer's Bride'.

Briefly explain each choice.

Language

The young wife is compared with nature to emphasise her youth, her natural innocence and energy, and her desire for freedom. These comparisons are expressed mainly in the form of **similes**.

She is 'flying like a hare'; 'like a mouse'; 'shy as a leveret'; 'straight as…'; 'sweet as…', and so on. The cattle, being real animals, are innocent and trusting 'like children'. (This also implies that she has the children that her husband yearns for.)

In this farming context, some of the **verbs** also contribute to the wife – nature comparison: she is 'chased' and 'caught', reminding us of traditional hunting activities.

The farmer might seem to deserve his 'punishment' of being shut out of his wife's thoughts and feelings, but he chose his wife in a traditional way: he had very little time or energy for choosing something as important as a wife, so he chose quickly. The farmer is not a cruel man, just naive and thoughtless. This is reflected in his **colloquial** (ordinary) language, the non-standard **dialect** of a simple farmer, for example: 'When us was wed'; 'she runned away'.

The farmer's absolute regret and disappointment (and perhaps also his unquestionable power over his wife) is strongly expressed through Mew's use of simple, contrasting colours: brown oaks; 'blue smoke'; 'grey sky'; 'black earth'; white frost. These cold colours contrast with the 'reddening berries' that symbolise the fertility and joy the farmer can never have.

Structure and form

Mew organises the poem around the farmer's first person narrative. This is what makes the poem compelling for the reader – a dramatic story being told in the voice of one character.

Throughout, the poem contrasts humans and nature. The farmer's wife bridges the gap between the two worlds and is consistently compared with animals and plants. This pattern of imagery is ironically reinforced when the wife is 'hunted' by the farmer and his neighbours.

Although the poem does stick to a regular rhythm, it does have highly rhythmic sections that draw attention to the wife's easy harmony with nature. For example:

> Shy as a leveret, swift as he,
> Straight and slight as a young larch tree…

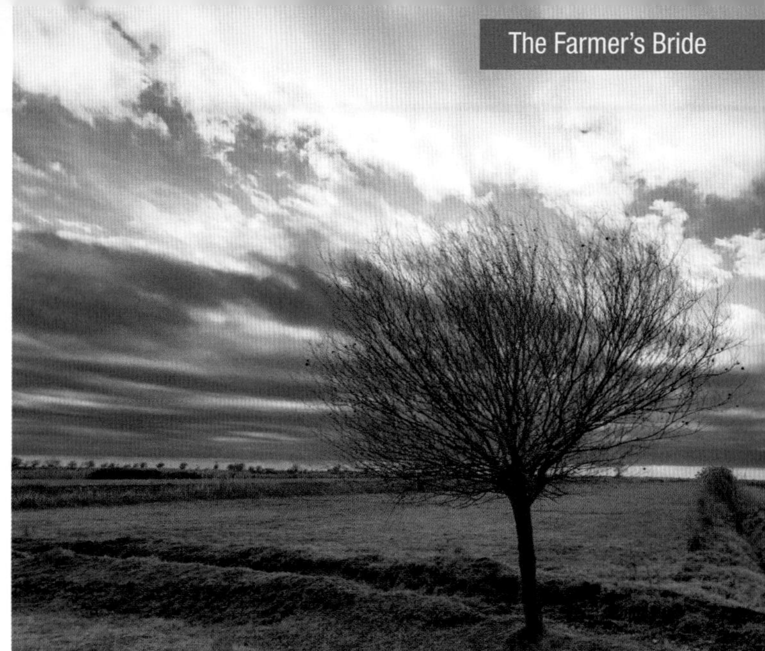

The regular placing of the stresses in these lines and the closeness of the rhymes creates a confident rhythm that suggests the natural strength of the wife. It also reminds us of the chorus of a folk song telling this sad story of the farmer and his bride.

Mew varies her rhyming to suit her purpose. For example, the last line of the first stanza is a sentence on its own but also the completion of a **rhyming couplet**, giving this moment – the wife's escape – dramatic emphasis. Mew even uses some rhyming triplets to strengthen the drama of moments in the narrative.

STRETCHIT!

Write a paragraph exploring how Mew uses rhythm and rhyme for effect in lines 38–41.

REVIEW IT!

1 For how long has the farmer been married?
2 When did the farmer's wife run away?
3 Why does Mew say the wife 'runned away' instead of 'ran away'?
4 List three words or phrases that suggest that the wife is trapped.
5 In the second stanza, what is suggested by the wife's 'wide brown stare'?
6 What is the wife like as a housekeeper?
7 Why is the farmer not enthusiastic about Christmas?
8 What colour is the wife's hair?
9 How do we feel about the farmer by the end of the poem?
10 Why do you think Mew repeats so many words in the final stanza?

DOIT!

- Add your own annotations to the poem, exploring more of its details and their effects. Include the underlined words or phrases.
- Online you will find a copy of the poem with more detailed annotations.

AQA exam-style question

Compare how poets present ideas about unequal relationships in 'The Farmer's Bride' and in one other poem from Love and relationships.

[30 marks]

Walking Away

Cecil Day-Lewis (1904–1972)

It is eighteen years ago, almost to the day –
A sunny day with leaves just turning,
The touch-lines new-ruled – since I watched you play
Your first game of football, then, like a satellite
Wrenched from its orbit, go drifting away

Behind a scatter of boys. I can see
You walking away from me towards the school
With the pathos of a half-fledged thing set free
Into a wilderness, the gait of one
Who finds no path where the path should be.

That hesitant figure, eddying away
Like a winged seed loosened from its parent stem,
Has something I never quite grasp to convey
About nature's give-and-take – the small, the scorching
Ordeals which fire one's irresolute clay.

I have had worse partings, but none that so
Gnaws at my mind still. Perhaps it is roughly
Saying what God alone could perfectly show –
How selfhood begins with a walking away,
And love is proved in the letting go.

Summary

This poem is from the point of view of a father whose son has grown up. The first line of the poem clearly lets us know that this is a memory from 'eighteen years ago' on a 'sunny day' in autumn and that the sports field has been newly marked. (Notice that these 'touch-lines' are 'new-ruled', symbolic of the new rules or guidelines in this parent/child relationship. See how the precise details help the reader to picture the scene.)

The boy is 'drifting', following a 'scatter of boys' away from his father. The father reflects that he is young ('half-fledged') and has yet to learn the way to go in life without his father's support. The father watches the child moving away and he finds it hard to explain how he feels. He knows that growing up is all part of nature, yet he finds his son's growing independence painful – a 'scorching/ Ordeal'. (Notice the images of moulding 'clay' that could suggest the events that shape lives. The father's ordeal is letting go – deciding to let go. His decision to let go has to be 'fired' by the reality of his son's walking away. Left to his own choice, he would never decide that his son was ready to go.)

The father reflects that he has had other 'worse' partings, but this one remains in his mind, 'gnaws'. (This is probably why the date and the setting is so clear in his mind in the first stanza.) He says that God will understand this feeling, as He had to let His son go too. The narrator reflects that when you love someone, you have to let them go. (This is the message of the poem.)

Context

Cecil Day-Lewis was Poet Laureate from 1968 to his death in 1972. The poem was dedicated to his son, Sean. It was written when Sean was an adult, but was set eighteen years before.

DEFINE IT!

convey – to tell, to pass on a message

eddying – to move in a circular way (usually describing water)

gait – the way someone walks

half-fledged – a baby bird that has grown some, but not all, of its flight feathers

irresolute – feeling undecided

ordeals – painful, unpleasant experiences

pathos – something that makes you feel sad or feel pity

satellite – at the time the poem was written this would have meant a planet or moon

touch-lines – markings on a sports field

Themes

Love: parent/child

The key message of the poem sums up the tension at the heart of parenting: if we love our children we have to let them go to live their own lives. Vivid and unsettling memories of that day still 'gnaw' at the narrator's mind.

Compare with
'Before You Were Mine': the narrator considers the life her mother lived before she was born.

Separation/letting go

The eventual separation of a parent/child relationship provides the core message of this poem. We can only become our true selves when we walk away and, as a parent, we show our love by 'letting go'.

Compare with
'Mother, any distance': the narrator anticipates breaking free from his mother.

Nature and the natural world

Love between father and son is seen as part of the natural world and its order. The boy, a 'winged seed' begins his journey, 'wrenched' from his father's 'orbit' to start his life. Autumn, 'with leaves just turning', signals change and ageing with 'nature's give and take'. Nature brings growth and maturity but breaks the parental bond.

Compare with
'Follower': the narrator follows his father working on the land. As an adult, he finds his father becomes his follower.

Language

The use of first person narrative gives an intimate, confessional tone. The narrator speaks directly to his son, 'Your first game of football', creating a sense of emotional intensity. This is reinforced by the precision in the date, 'It is eighteen years ago, almost to the day' and detailed setting, 'touch-lines new-ruled'. The repeated 'Away' echoes throughout, adding to the melancholy. Word choices 'Gnaws', 'pathos' 'wrenched' 'scorching/ ordeals' add to the sense of pain.

The violence of the 'satellite/wrenched' suggests alarm as the father realises his son is moving away from him following an unpredictable 'scatter of boys'. Images of natural movement continue with 'eddying away', 'winged seed'.

STRETCH IT!

In a letter to *The Guardian* newspaper, Sean Day-Lewis said:

> "The poem, as it happens, was dedicated to me, but I guarantee that whenever I am asked to give a public reading, mine are not the only wet eyes."

Why do you think the poem continues to have an emotional appeal?

Structure and form

The poem is written in five five-line stanzas, with a regular ABACA rhyme-scheme which supports the poem steady walking pace and reflective tone.

To explore the poem's narrative structure, try to write no more than five words to sum up the purpose of each stanza.

Stanza one might be summed up as: 'introduces a significant memory'.

1 When is the poem set?
2 Where is the poem set?
3 How do we know that the father often thinks of this moment?
4 We are told that the son walks 'Behind a scatter of boys'. Explain what this suggests about the father's hold over his son.
5 What does 'half-fledged' mean?
6 How does Day-Lewis describe the son in stanza three?
7 What is the effect of the word 'wrenched'?
8 What is the effect of the repeated use of 'away' in the poem?
9 What is the message of the poem?
10 What does the father remember about the way the son walked away?

- Add your own annotations to the poem, exploring more of its details and their effects. Include the underlined words or phrases.
- Online you will find a copy of the poem with more detailed annotations.

AQA exam-style question

Compare how poets present parenthood in 'Walking Away' and in one other poem from Love and relationships.

[30 marks]

Eden Rock

Charles Causley (1917–2003)

They are waiting for me somewhere beyond Eden Rock:
My father, twenty-five, in the same suit
Of Genuine Irish Tweed, his terrier Jack
Still two years old and trembling at his feet.

My mother, twenty-three, in a sprigged dress
Drawn at the waist, ribbon in her straw hat,
Has spread the stiff white cloth over the grass.
Her hair, the colour of wheat, takes on the light.

She pours tea from a Thermos, the milk straight
From an old H.P. sauce bottle, a screw
Of paper for a cork; slowly sets out
The same three plates, the tin cups painted blue.

The sky whitens as if lit by three suns.
My mother shades her eyes and looks my way
Over the drifted stream. My father spins
A stone along the water. Leisurely,

They beckon to me from the other bank.
I hear them call, 'See where the stream-path is!
Crossing is not as hard as you might think.'

I had not thought that it would be like this.

Summary

The narrator imagines his dead parents still waiting for him 'beyond Eden Rock', just as they were in a memory he describes for us. In this memory his father is 25, in his tweed suit, with his dog 'trembling at his feet'. (Why is the dog 'trembling'? Is he cold after swimming? Is he frightened of his owner?)

His mother, 23, is wearing a summer dress and hat, and is spreading a white cloth on the ground. Her fair hair shines in the sun. (Notice the sharp, bright descriptions that are easy to imagine.)

She pours tea from a Thermos flask, and milk from a clean 'H.P. sauce bottle' which has screwed-up 'paper for a cork'. She sets out plates and cups for a picnic. (The parents seem not to be rich. This was a time before disposable plastic containers and when it was still normal for a man to wear a suit on a picnic, but the parents do improvise a milk container, and they have painted their tin cups to restore them rather than replacing them.)

The day gets brighter and very white. The narrator's mother shades her eyes and looks across the stream at him. His father is skimming stones. (The whiteness of the day and the picnic cloth, and the brightness of the mother's hair might suggest that the narrator is both remembering the past and seeing a vision of his parents in heaven.)

Relaxed, his parents 'beckon' the narrator and urge him to cross the stream to them. The narrator remarks that he 'had not thought it would be like this'. (The last line – and the whole poem – is simple, beautiful and mysterious. Probably how a reader interprets the last word, 'this', will be a key to their understanding of the whole poem.)

DEFINE IT!

Irish tweed – a closely woven woollen fabric of high quality

sprigged – fabric decorated with small flowers or leaves

DO IT!

Here is one possible explanation of Causley's word, 'this':

His parents encouraging him to die too so as to be reunited with them.

Write down at least two other simple explanations for 'this'.

STRETCH IT!

Explain what you think the poem's final line means.

Context

Causley was an only child. His father died when he was very young. In the Bible, Eden is a paradise where the first humans, Adam and Eve, lived. Charles Causley says there is no real place called Eden Rock: he made it up.

Themes

Parents

The narrator's parents beckon to him and encourage him but they are not described as though they love him deeply. They seem relaxed and distant, and although he describes them clearly they seem very self-contained.

Compare with
'Follower': the narrator wants to distance himself from his father.

'Before You Were Mine'

Regrets and nostalgia

The last line could be read as regretful and disappointed, although it is ambiguous. The narrator's nostalgia for the perfect day at the paradise of Eden Rock is strongly suggested in the clear and beautiful descriptions.

Compare with
'Neutral Tones': the narrator reinterprets an incident in the past with a sense of bitterness.

'Walking Away'

Connection (and disconnection)

His parents are 'waiting for' the narrator and they seem to want to be reunited with him. However, the stream divides them.

Compare with
'Mother, any distance': here, the narrator anticipates breaking free from his mother but remaining connected.

DO IT!

Choose two more themes relevant to 'Eden Rock' and to Love and relationships.

For each theme, list one more poem that you could compare with 'Eden Rock'.

Briefly explain each of your choices.

Language

The language is simple and economical. Causley chooses many monosyllabic words – especially verbs such as 'drawn', 'spread', 'pours'. This makes the descriptions sharp and believable. Causley uses colloquial language such as 'takes on' and 'sets out' to emphasise his parents' ordinariness. His imagery avoids similes and metaphors in favour of straightforward, literal descriptions – like photograph snapshots – which present the scene precisely so that it is easy for the reader to see in their mind.

DO IT!

Choose one other descriptive detail in the poem and briefly explore its effect on the reader.

See how this student explores language in the second stanza, making a clear point, and choosing evidence precisely:

> Using only literal description, Causley makes the picnic cloth both beautiful and very real: the cloth is simply 'stiff' and 'white'. This allows the reader to make their own associations: perhaps 'stiff' hints at coldness and even death, while 'white' might suggest purity, but coldness too.

Structure and form

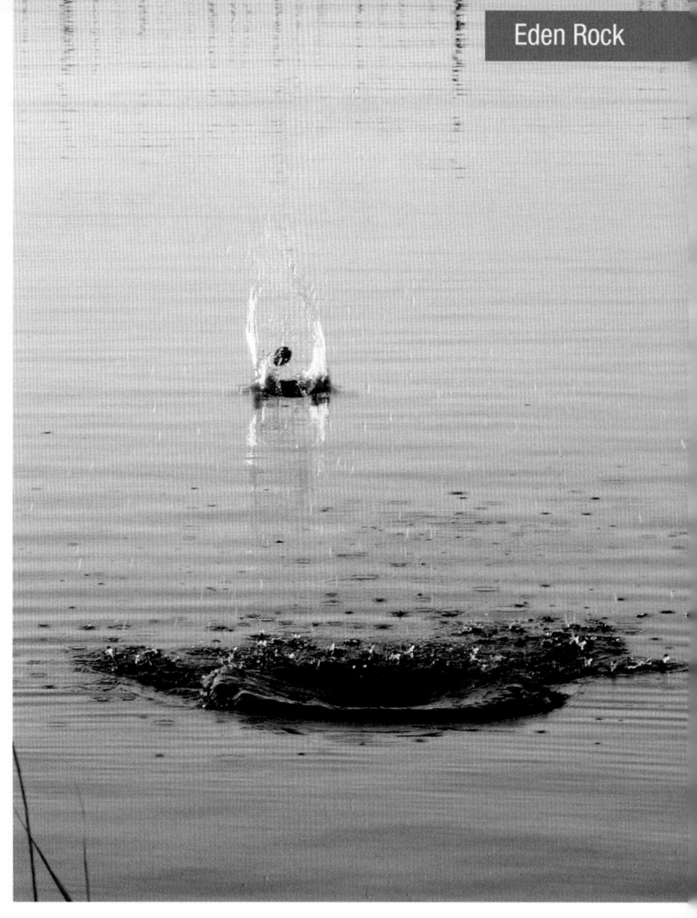

The narrative of the picnic at Eden Rock is what gives the poem its structure – the descriptive details, the dialogue, the characters (the parents) and the chronology of events. Other structural features include the consistent patterns of language (see page 48). These elements give the poem coherence and a quiet dramatic momentum, culminating in the final, isolated line that can be considered as an anticlimax in that Causley's conclusion is ambiguous.

The momentum of the poem is supported by its regular rhyme scheme (in each stanza, lines one and three and two and four rhyme) and the even lengths of its lines (most of them have ten syllables). On the other hand, to respect the personal, reflective mood of the poem, Causley uses near rhymes rather than full rhymes, and an irregular metre, so that the reader can linger over details, rather than gallop to the end.

1. How much older than his mother is the narrator's father?
2. What is his father wearing?
3. What is his mother wearing?
4. What pattern is on his mother's clothes?
5. Why are the parents at Eden Rock?
6. Why do the narrator's parents 'beckon' to him?
7. What is the poem's rhyme scheme?
8. Why do you think Causley used half rather than full rhymes?
9. What do you think is the most likely meaning of the word, 'it', in the final line?
10. What do you think the narrator's parents mean when they say that 'Crossing is not as hard as you might think.'?

- Add your own annotations to the poem, exploring more of its details and their effects. Include the underlined words or phrases.
- Online you will find a copy of the poem with more detailed annotations.

AQA exam-style question

Compare how poets present attitudes towards parents (or a parent) in 'Eden Rock' and in one other poem from Love and relationships.

[30 marks]

Follower

Seamus Heaney (1939–2013)

My father worked with a horse-plough,
His shoulders globed like a full sail strung
Between the shafts and the furrow.
The horse strained at his clicking tongue.

An expert. He would set the wing
And fit the bright steel-pointed sock.
The sod rolled over without breaking.
At the headrig, with a single pluck

Of reins, the sweating team turned round
And back into the land. His eye
Narrowed and angled at the ground,
Mapping the furrow exactly.

I stumbled in his hob-nailed wake,
Fell sometimes on the polished sod;
Sometimes he rode me on his back
Dipping and rising to his plod.

I wanted to grow up and plough,
To close one eye, stiffen my arm.
All I ever did was follow
In his broad shadow round the farm.

I was a nuisance, tripping, falling,
Yapping always. But today
It is my father who keeps stumbling
Behind me, and will not go away.

Summary

Heaney remembers his father ploughing fields, and how well he kept the horses under control. (The description of his father as a sailing ship conveys how large he appeared to be in comparison with Heaney as a small boy. Heaney seems to be in awe of his father.)

Heaney calls his father an expert who works the plough in a precise way, trusting his eye to 'map' the ploughing exactly. (The technical terms used by Heaney strengthen the impression of his father's expertise.)

Heaney remembers himself stumbling and falling as he follows his father, and how his father would sometimes carry him on his back. (His father's movement – 'dipping and rising' – reinforces the image of him as a ship on an ocean.)

Heaney's ambition was to be an expert ploughman like his father, but as a child he could only follow. (He follows literally 'in his broad shadow': he is overshadowed by his father.)

When Heaney was a child he got in his father's way; he 'was a nuisance', but now – grown up with his own career – he sees his father as a burden that 'will not go away'. (Note that Heaney says 'will not' rather than *does* not. It is as if he has asked his father to leave him alone.)

DEFINE IT!

furrow – a planting trench made by a plough

headrig – a large mechanical saw for cutting up logs

plough – a farming tool pulled by a horse (or tractor) to turn over earth ready for planting

sock – part of a plough

sod – soil, earth

wing – part of a plough

Context

Heaney grew up on a farm in Northern Ireland. He had eight brothers and sisters. By the time 'Follower' was published in 1966, Heaney was a university teacher.

Here is a student making *helpful* use of contextual information:

> By the time 'Follower' was published in 1966, Heaney had a highly skilled career of his own. The childhood worship of his father expressed in 'Follower' is replaced by a sense that his father is now as much a hindrance to his life, as he was to his father's. Their roles have reversed.

Themes

Parents

Heaney wants to be his father's 'follower', showing how much he looks up to him. He admires his father, and he appreciates his skills with a close attention to detail. However, when Heaney becomes an independent adult the roles are reversed and Heaney is burdened – perhaps haunted – by his father.

Compare with
'Before You Were Mine': the narrator seems to prefer a past version of her mother.

'Eden Rock'

Admiration and worship

Heaney wants to be his father's 'follower' as though his father is a god. Heaney's admiration is almost a form of worship.

Compare with
'Porphyria's Lover': the narrator wants Porphyria to 'worship' him.

'Climbing My Grandfather'

Breaking away

Through most of the memory in the poem, Heaney is tied to his father. Finally, though, he is eager to break away, even rejecting his father.

Compare with
'Mother, any distance': here the narrator anticipates breaking free from his mother but not rejecting her.

Language

The language is simple and economical to reflect the precise, practical way that Heaney's father ploughed. Heaney uses precise verbs ('strained', 'rolled'), and very few **adjectives**. The few he does use tend to be factual ('clicking', 'sweating', 'steel-pointed') rather than decorative. The whole poem's plain style is set up by the very factual first line.

Heaney does use some metaphors to express the awe the young Heaney feels for his father: an extended metaphor develops an image of Heaney's father as a ship in full sail, riding the waves: his shoulders are 'globed like a full sail', he 'dips and rises' as he ploughs, leaving his son in his 'wake' (the frothy water a boat leaves behind). For creating a mood of almost religious awe, these images are more effective than the mainly ordinary, plain language of the poem.

Structure and form

The poem is organised around Heaney's precise account of his father's work and the equipment used for it. At points this account is interrupted by a lesson to be drawn from it: that his father is an obvious expert; that his father's expertise inspires Heaney with the ambition to become a ploughman too. As well as a precise account of ploughing, the poem is also an **allegory** of father–son relationships: Heaney as a boy struggles to live up to his father's standards (he 'stumbles' behind him); as an older man, his father now 'keeps stumbling/Behind' Heaney. He now depends on Heaney who resents his dependence. This 'about turn' is a dramatic point in the poem structure.

The poem's momentum is supported by its regular rhyme scheme (in each stanza, lines one and three and two and four rhyme) and the roughly even lengths of its lines. On the other hand, to suit the thoughtful, personal nature of Heaney's memory, he often uses near (or 'half') rhymes rather than full ones, and the lines do not have a brisk rhythm. These features restrain the poem's momentum, allowing the reader to notice details, but also to read through evenly, without 'stumbling'. The form of the poem is like the father's ploughing – even and confident but not 'flashy'.

To explore the poem's narrative structure, try to write *no more than five words* to sum up the purpose of each stanza.

Stanza one might be summed up as: 'Clear picture of father ploughing'.

1 How does Heaney's father control the horses?
2 How do we know he skilfully turns the horse at the end of the furrow?
3 How does the father show his expertise in stanza three?
4 What does Heaney remember doing in the second half of stanza four?
5 Which four words in stanza five most clearly show Heaney's sense of failure?
6 What does Heaney mean by calling himself 'a nuisance'?
7 What is the poem's rhyme scheme?
8 Why do you think Heaney used half rather than full rhymes?
9 In the final line, what is the effect of the words 'will not'?
10 Why do you think Heaney called his poem 'Follower'?

- Add your own annotations to the poem, exploring more of its details and their effects. Include the underlined words or phrases.
- Online you will find a copy of the poem with more detailed annotations.

AQA exam-style question

Compare how poets present family bonds in 'Follower' and in one other poem from Love and relationships.

[30 marks]

Mother, any distance

Simon Armitage (b.1963)

From *Book of Matches*

Mother, any distance greater than a single span
requires a second pair of hands.
You come to help me measure windows, pelmets, doors,
the acres of the walls, the prairies of the floors.

You at the zero-end, me with the spool of tape, recording
length, reporting metres, centimetres back to base, then leaving
up the stairs, the line still feeding out, unreeling
years between us. Anchor. Kite.

I space-walk through the empty bedrooms, climb
the ladder to the loft, to breaking point, where something
has to give;
two floors below your fingertips still pinch
the last one-hundredth of an inch ... I reach
towards a hatch that opens on an endless sky
to fall or fly.

Summary

This poem is from the point of view of a man as he illustrates and explores his relationship with his mother. The poem begins by the son addressing his mother directly. The mother is helping him measure up what we assume is his new home. (Notice the 'acres' of the walls and 'prairies' of the floors, suggesting childhood games, but also exploration and adventure.)

The narrator (the son) describes this measuring process, but the focus shifts as the mother is seen as the 'zero-end' of the tape measure and his 'base'. There is obvious affection in his descriptions. (An extended metaphor of a range of things tethered to a fixed point suggests the mother/child bond through the umbilical cord: the cord that attaches the baby to the placenta during pregnancy.)

The metaphor of the 'space-walk' continues to show the bond between the mother and son, but the need to move away is introduced as 'something has to give'. The reader understands that this is part of the growing-up process. The mother still holds on to the tape measure – but it is 'the last one-hundredth of an inch' of the tape that is at full stretch. The son decisively reaches out to the loft hatch that opens to 'an endless sky'. (The metaphor shows the loft hatch as freedom and independence. There also might be a play on the word 'hatch' with associations of birds hatching, growing.) The final line is ambiguous, 'to fall or fly' – leaving the reader with the question, will this be successful, or not?

DEFINE IT!

acres – a measurement of land

pelmets – a narrow border of wood or cloth used to hide curtain tracks at a window

prairies – a large open area of grassland usually in America

space-walk – an activity outside a spacecraft undertaken by an astronaut

spool of tape – a tape measure that is wound into a circle

unreeling – to unwind

DO IT!

1 Look up images of a tape measure, an astronaut doing a space-walk, a kite, an anchor. Look at the images. What do they all have in common? Why do you think Armitage uses these images?

2 Look at 'Anchor. Kite'.
What words or phrases do you associate with these words? Try to think of at least three associations for each word.

STRETCH IT!

The ending is ambiguous: 'to fall or fly'. What do you understand by this line?

Context

'Mother, any distance' is taken from Simon Armitage's *Book of Matches*. The poem is taken from the first section, a group of 30 sonnets. Each poem is intended to be read in the time taken for a lit match to burn out (around 20 seconds).

Themes

Love: parent/child

Addressed to his mother, the son's attachment to his mother is clear despite his need to move to adulthood. His mother 'helps' him and provides his 'base', his support.

Compare with
'Before You Were Mine': the narrator admires the life her mother lived before she was born.

Distance/letting go

The eventual separation of a parent/child relationship underpins the core message of this poem. We can only become our true selves when we 'fall or fly' and gain our independence through an 'endless sky'.

Compare with
'Walking Away': the father considers the loss of his son as he grows up.

Family ties

Love between mother and son is implicit through their actions – she is there for any 'distance' that requires a 'second pair of hands'. The son is tethered to her through a series of images: she is the 'zero-end', he is at the other end of the spool of tape like the umbilical cord attaching the unborn baby to the mother within the womb.

Compare with
'Climbing My Grandfather': the grandson's love for his grandfather.

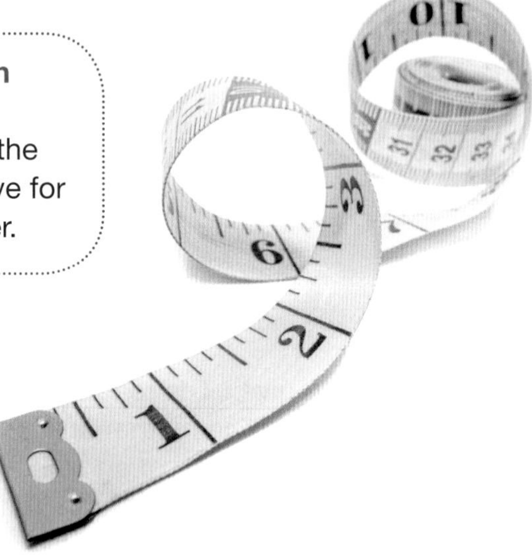

Language

The language of the poem is straightforward and its simplicity allows Armitage to define the multi-layered love and connection between a mother and a child. His wordplay helps him to explore the tensions as well as the connections: 'anchor' suggests stability and security yet can also seem weighty and restricting; a 'kite' is free and airy, yet is held in one place securely, restricting its freedom; the tape is 'unreeling' letting out, exploring, yet this word can also suggest being out of control.

See how this student explores imagery in the poem, making a clear point, and chooses evidence precisely before showing why this is important to the reader's understanding:

> Armitage uses the extended image of the tape to show the relationship between the mother and son. The son is seen as the explorer as he 'space-walks' through the house, unravelling the 'spool of tape'. Despite his need for freedom, the reader understands that the tape is anchored by the mother in a similar way to their original bond, the umbilical cord.

Choose one other detail in the poem and briefly explore its meaning and effect.

Structure and form

A sonnet is about self-restraint. 'Mother, any distance' is about the fearful assertion of freedom, so the poem looks like a sonnet, but isn't. Just as the narrator strains at the boundaries of the house and of his childhood, Armitage strains at the boundaries of a sonnet.

The poem is held together by the idea of a connection just held on to across distance ('to breaking point') and specifically the extended image of the tape measure.

The poem's rhythm is relatively regular in the first stanza as the mother and son work together to 'measure' up. Halfway through the second stanza, as the son begins to explore his boundaries further, line length and rhythm become irregular, reflecting the disruption to the mother/child connection that is being maintained solely by the mother's 'fingertips'. This connection is strained further before the ellipsis (…) signals a pause in their struggle, but it fails to restrain his movement to 'reach/towards a hatch'. This movement, split between the two lines, shows the son's struggle and determination to make this move.

1 Who is the narrator addressing directly in the poem?
2 What measurement requires 'a second pair of hands'?
3 The son reports 'back to base'. Who is the base?
4 What is meant by 'You at the zero end'?
5 Why are the bedrooms empty?
6 Who is the anchor, and who is the kite? Briefly explain your answer.
7 How is this sonnet different to the traditional sonnet form?
8 How is this sonnet's subject different to the traditional sonnet subject matter?
9 What does the ellipsis (…) signal in line 13?
10 How does Armitage use language to show the complicated nature of parent/child relationships?

- Add your own annotations to the poem, exploring more of its details and their effects. Include the underlined words or phrases.
- Online you will find a copy of the poem with more detailed annotations.

AQA exam-style question

Compare how poets present a struggle for growing independence in 'Mother, any distance' and in one other poem from Love and relationships.

[30 marks]

Before You Were Mine

Carol Ann Duffy (b.1955)

I'm ten years away from the corner you laugh on
with your pals, Maggie McGeeney and Jean Duff.
The three of you bend from the waist, holding
each other, or your knees, and shriek at the pavement.
Your polka-dot dress blows round your legs. Marilyn.

I'm not here yet. The thought of me doesn't occur
in the ballroom with the thousand eyes, the fizzy, movie tomorrows
the right walk home could bring. I knew you would dance
like that. Before you were mine, your Ma stands at the close
with a hiding for the late one. You reckon it's worth it.

The decade ahead of my loud, possessive yell was the best one, eh?
I remember my hands in those high-heeled red shoes, relics,
and now your ghost clatters toward me over George Square
till I see you, clear as scent, under the tree,
with its lights, and whose small bites on your neck, sweetheart?

Cha cha cha! You'd teach me the steps on the way home from Mass,
stamping stars from the wrong pavement. Even then
I wanted the bold girl winking in Portobello, somewhere
in Scotland, before I was born. That glamorous love lasts
where you sparkle and waltz and laugh before you were mine.

Summary

The narrator presents a celebration of her mother's early life in this poem – a time 'ten years' before the narrator's birth – through a series of snapshots of small moments. The mother is laughing with two friends on a street corner in a spotted dress. (Notice how her happiness and youth are presented through 'laugh', 'pals', 'shriek'.)

The next scene is in a ballroom. The narrator states that at this moment the mother hasn't 'thought' of having a child. The mother is dancing and thinks it is worth staying to dance despite the punishment for being late. (Notice the freedom and the excitement of 'fizzy, movie tomorrows' and how it is overshadowed by 'I'm not here yet'.)

The scene shifts to the narrator playing with her mother's shoes as a small child. Then moves again to the mother's past, where she is shown under a Christmas tree in George Square with 'small bites' on her neck. (Notice the precise setting, the sexuality suggested by both the red shoes and the lovebites.)

The final scene is again on a pavement, but this time the narrator is returning home from Mass with her mother. Despite being a small child, she yearns for the 'bold girl' and the glamour of her mother's past. (Notice how she sees the difference between the mother who had 'sparkle' and the parent who no longer has that.)

DEFINE IT!

cha cha cha – a Latin ballroom dance

close – a street with a dead end

George Square – a square in the centre of Glasgow, Scotland

hiding – a colloquial term for smack/ punishment

Ma – a colloquial name for mother

Mass – a regular Roman Catholic church service

Marilyn – reference to Marilyn Monroe a famous film star

polka dot – spotted

Portobello – part of Edinburgh, Scotland

relic – something left over from the past, often with religious significance

waltz – a ballroom dance

STRETCH IT!

What is the tone of 'The decade ahead of my loud, possessive yell was the best one, eh?' Explain your ideas.

DO IT!

Explain what Duffy means by 'the ballroom with the thousand eyes'.

Context

References to the ballroom and the dances 'waltz' and 'Cha cha cha' as well as the references to glamour, movies and Marilyn Monroe, set the mother's past in the 1950s. These references place the mother in Glasgow in this 'fizzy' and 'glamorous' time.

Themes

Love: parent/child

Addressed to her mother, the daughter's admiration of her mother is clearly shown through the glamour associated with dance, movie and movie star images used throughout.

Compare with
'Mother any distance': the narrator anticipates breaking away from his mother.

Parenthood

The reader considers the life our parents lived before we were born and how their lives had to change once we were there.

Compare with
'Eden Rock': nostalgic snapshot of the narrator's parents and a family picnic.

DO IT!

Find one more theme relevant to 'Before You Were Mine' and to Love and relationships.

For the theme, list one more poem that you could compare with 'Before You Were Mine'.

Briefly explain your choice.

Time

The poem explores the time before the narrator was born, her mother's teenage years; the present day and the narrator's childhood.

Compare with
'When We Two Parted': set in three time frames, the poem explores the breakdown of a relationship.

Language

The narrator is nostalgic for the romance of her mother's youth citing 'the fizzy, movie tomorrows' with the heady promise of what love could bring through 'the right walk home'. These are idealised memories, vivid snapshots appealing to the senses as 'clear as scent' (with reference here to the link between scent and memory), 'Your polka dot dress blows round your legs', 'your ghost clatters toward me'.

Word choices highlight youthful liveliness and joy – as well as hinting at youthful rebellion. We are shown the 'lovebites', we almost hear the mother's teenage voice – 'You reckon it's worth it' – when a 'hiding' is threatened 'for a late one'.

The child's possessive language, 'Before you were mine', echoes through the poem, both starting it through the title and ending it. Possession here is a surprising reversal of the parent/child relationship. Here it is the child who possesses the parent. Here we hear the baby's 'loud possessive yell' and are told that she 'wanted the bold girl winking in Portobello'.

Structure

The structure and coherence of the poem comes through the presentation of a series of images – almost like snapshots or short movies – suggesting that the narrator is looking through a photograph album and reconstructing memories, real or imagined. The events in the poem start and end with an image of a pavement. The first image is full of joyous laughter; the second still has the joy of dance but it is tinged with regret: 'Even then/I wanted the bold girl'.

The poem is written in four five-line stanzas and the lack of rhyme and of end-stopped lines gives the poem a conversational tone that is reinforced by the direct address to the mother. Within each stanza there are shifts of time and place. In stanzas one and two the time is before the narrator's birth, but the narrator is commenting on this in the present. In stanzas three and four, we see the mother's past and the narrator's childhood. We are shown the responsibility of parenthood, the red shoes that are cast off and used as toys as they become 'relics', and the loss of the 'bold girl' who would 'sparkle and waltz and laugh'.

1. Who is the poem addressed to?
2. Who are Maggie McGeeney and Jean Duff?
3. Who is 'Marilyn'?
4. Find a quotation to show the tension between the mother and the grandmother.
5. Where is the poem mostly set?
6. What clues are we given that the mother was rebellious?
7. What dance does the mother teach the child?
8. Find a quotation to suggest that the mother does not wear the red shoes after the narrator is born.
9. What clues are we given about how the mother had changed in the final stanza?
10. Is the mother alive or dead? Explain your ideas.

- Add your own annotations to the poem, exploring more of its details and their effects. Include the underlined words or phrases.
- Online you will find a copy of the poem with more detailed annotations.

AQA exam-style question

Compare how poets present the power of memories in 'Before You Were Mine' and in one other poem from Love and relationships.

[30 marks]

Winter Swans

Owen Sheers (b.1974)

The clouds had given their all –
two days of rain and then a break
in which we walked,

the waterlogged earth
gulping for breath at our feet
as we skirted the lake, silent and apart,

until the swans came and stopped us
with a show of tipping in unison.
As if rolling weights down their bodies to their heads

they halved themselves in the dark water,
icebergs of white feather, paused before returning again
like boats righting in rough weather.

'They mate for life' you said as they left,
porcelain over the stilling water. I didn't reply
but as we moved on through the afternoon light,

slow-stepping in the lake's shingle and sand,
I noticed our hands, that had, somehow,
swum the distance between us

and folded, one over the other,
like a pair of wings settling after flight.

Summary

A couple out on a winter walk are brought closer together through their shared observation of some swans. (Perhaps Sheers chooses to set the poem in winter to emphasise the cold and cheerless state of the couple's relationship.)

After two days of solid rain, a couple go for a walk round a lake. They are 'silent and apart' until the swans arrive and start upending themselves in the water, probably as part of a courtship ritual. (Note how nature is wet, soggy and discouraging while the white swans contrast with this. They are the focus that begins to bring the two people together.)

The swans come up for air, righting themselves. One of the human couple remarks that swan couples stay together 'for life'. The other person doesn't reply but notices that he (or she) has moved closer to their partner, and that their hands join like 'wings settling after flight'. (Presumably the swans' unity has inspired the couple, and their own new togetherness happens unconsciously, automatically.)

DEFINE IT!

iceberg – a huge block of ice floating in the sea, with much of its bulk below the water

porcelain – sometimes called 'fine china'; a strong, thin, beautiful material used for making delicate jugs, bowls, etc.

shingle – a mass of very small stones

skirted – moved round the edge

unison – together, as one

Context

Most swans have only one partner for life. They are admired for their serene, effortless swimming and for the beautiful white reflections they make in ponds and lakes.

It is conventional in many societies to talk about emotional as well as physical distance.

See how one student deals with this aspect of the poem's context and draws on their wider knowledge in a way that enriches their understanding:

> When relationships break down, sometimes one partner complains that the other has gone 'cold' and 'distant'. At the beginning of the poem the couple are walking 'apart', but this is caused by them being 'apart' emotionally. Their interaction with the swans is a healing process, closing the physical and therefore the emotional 'distance between' them.

Themes

Distance and separation

At first the lovers are 'silent and apart'. By the end of the poem, 'the distance between' them has been closed. They are holding hands.

Compare with
'Eden Rock': the stream divides the narrator from his parents.

'Neutral Tones': the coldness of winter.

Togetherness

The swans are together: they work 'in unison'. The human couple realise that the swans stay together for life, and this inspires them to reunite.

Compare with
'Letters from Yorkshire': distance is overcome by communication and the union of 'souls'.

'Climbing My Grandfather'

Nature

The coldness of the season – winter – seems to echo the humans' emotional coldness. The swans, however, offer an inspiring model of faithfulness and cooperation.

Compare with
'Walking Away': lessons from nature and its 'give-and-take'.

'Neutral Tones'

Language

The narrator sees the swans in a variety of ways which help him to understand his own relationship and how to improve it. For example, in representing them as icebergs, he realises that a relationship is deeper and more substantial than it might appear at any given moment. The swans are also 'porcelain', suggesting the precious nature of a relationship and the care it needs if it is to survive. The simile of the swans as 'boats righting in rough weather' reminds him that relationships can become turbulent, but that couples – like swans – can, and should, 'right themselves'. Through this accumulation of imagery, Owen Sheers presents the swans' behaviour as a lesson for improved human behaviour. By the end of the poem, the humans' hands become 'a pair of wings' so that the humans are united with each other and with the swans.

Explain why Sheers uses the image of 'the waterlogged earth/ gulping for breath at our feet'.

Never just mention a technique a poet has used (for example, **alliteration**, personification, etc.). Always explore the technique's *effect* on the reader.

Structure and form

A number of structural features give the poem a feeling of coherence and completeness. The stanzas are ragged in shape and rhythm and have three lines each – an odd number that perhaps suggests the 'oddness' – as well as the raggedness – of the couple's relationship. However, the poem charts a journey from separation to togetherness: at first the couple are 'silent and apart', then the swans arrive and suggest positive lessons to the couple, breaking their silence ('They mate for life'). Finally, the distance between the couple closes in a joining of hands.

STRETCH IT!

How might the physical shape of the poem – how it looks on the page – help its meaning?

NAIL IT!

Only mention a poem's structural features – for example, rhythm, stanzas, etc. – if you are going to explore how those features support the poem's meaning and effect.

For example:

The final stanza of 'Winter Swans' breaks the pattern of three-line stanzas. The final stanza is a couplet, emphasising the couple's new-found togetherness.

REVIEW IT!

1 Is it raining when the couple go for their walk?
2 What do the couple say to each other at the start of the poem?
3 What made the couple stop?
4 What do the swans' feathers make them look like while they 'tip'?
5 What information about swans does the narrator's partner give?
6 What does the narrator notice as they walk on?
7 What simile does the narrator use for their hands?
8 Name two things that give the poem a sense of shape and completeness.
9 What is meant by the line, 'they halved themselves'?
10 Do you think the couple will stay together? Briefly explain your thoughts.

DO IT!

- Add your own annotations to the poem, exploring more of its details and their effects. Include the underlined words or phrases.
- Online you will find a copy of the poem with more detailed annotations.

AQA exam-style question

Compare how poets present separation and/or togetherness in 'Winter Swans' and in one other poem from Love and relationships.

[30 marks]

Singh Song!

Daljit Nagra (b. 1966)

I run just one ov my daddy's shops
from 9 o'clock to 9 o'clock
and he vunt me not to hav a break
but ven nobody in, I do di lock –

cos up di stairs is my newly bride
vee share in chapatti
vee share in di chutney
after vee hav made luv
like vee rowing through Putney –

Ven I return vid my pinnie untied
di shoppers always point and cry:
Hey Singh, ver yoo bin?
Yor lemons are limes
yor bananas are plantain,
dis dirty little floor need a little bit of mop
in di worst Indian shop
on di whole Indian road –

Above my head high heel tap di ground
as my vife on di web is playing wid di mouse
ven she netting two cat on her Sikh lover site
she book dem for di meat at di cheese ov her price –

my bride
she effing at my mum
in all di colours of Punjabi
den stumble like a drunk
making fun at my daddy

my bride
tiny eyes ov a gun
and di tummy ov a teddy

my bride
she hav a red crew cut
and she wear a Tartan sari
a donkey jacket and some pumps
on di squeak ov di girls dat are pinching my sweeties –

Ven I return from di tickle ov my bride
di shoppers always point and cry:
Hey Singh, ver yoo bin?
Di milk is out ov date
and di bread is alvays stale,
di tings yoo hav on offer yoo hav never got in stock
in di worst Indian shop
on di whole Indian road –

Late in di midnight hour
ven yoo shoppers are wrap up quiet
ven di precinct is concrete-cool
vee cum down whispering stairs
and sit on my silver stool,
from behind di chocolate bars
vee stare past di half-price window signs
at di beaches ov di UK in di brightey moon –

from di stool each night she say,
How much do yoo charge for dat moon baby?

from di stool each night I say,
Is half di cost ov yoo baby,

from di stool each night she say,
How much does dat come to baby?

from di stool each night I say,
Is priceless baby –

Summary

The narrator tells us that he runs one of his father's shops. His father doesn't like him having a break, but when he has no customers he locks the door and goes upstairs to his new wife. They eat together and make love vigorously. (The narrator rebels against his father's wishes.) When he goes back downstairs, angry shoppers ask where he's been and accuse him of keeping a dirty shop with poor produce. (They are right, but the narrator dreams of doing something more exciting than running a shop.)

Upstairs his wife is working on the Sikh dating site she has set up. The narrator says that his wife likes to mock his father, but he loves her eyes and her cuddly belly. She is a rebel who has a 'red crew cut' and wears tartan under a donkey jacket, with pumps on her feet. She catches shoplifters. (His wife is outspoken and independent, and he loves that.)

In the cool evenings after the shop shuts, the narrator and his wife sit behind the counter, looking out through the window at pictures in a travel agent opposite. When she asks him how much he would charge for the bright moon, he teases her by telling her she costs him twice as much. When she presses him to give an exact price, he tells her she is 'priceless'. (The narrator seems entranced by his wife. He is very romantic, moonlight being a traditional companion to romance.)

DEFINE IT!

chapatti – a flatbread eaten by many Indians

crew cut – very short hair

donkey jacket – a dark heavy jacket typically worn by building workers

pinnie – a shopkeeper's apron

plantain – a fruit that looks like a green, under-ripe banana

priceless – too valuable to have a price

pumps – plimsolls, daps, light shoes

Punjabi – the language spoken by most Sikhs in India

Putney – an area of London next to the River Thames

sari – an Indian dress that wraps around the waist and over one shoulder

Sikh – a person who follows the Sikh religion

Singh – all male Sikhs include Singh in their name

tartan – a criss-cross pattern associated with Scotland

Context

Daljit Nagra's parents were Sikhs. Like many immigrants from India, they ran a grocery shop in Britain. The poem tries to represent the true voice of a recent Indian immigrant.

NAIL IT!

Context is only relevant if it sheds light on the poem and your exam question. Look at these two students' comments on context. The first is useful; the second is not.

Student Answer A

'Singh Song!' tries to copy the sound of the voice of a recent Indian immigrant like Nagra's own father. Clearly Nagra wants us to enjoy the sound of that voice - the voice of his father, not mock it.

Student Answer B

Daljit Nagra's parents owned a shop.

Themes

Family

The narrator has his own wife, but he is under the control of his father who is his employer. The narrator's behaviour is a rebellion against this control by a father he calls 'daddy' as though he is a child still. He admires his wife's open defiance of his father.

Compare with
'Eden Rock'

'Walking Away': the father is reluctant to stop controlling his son.

Romance and passion

The narrator and his wife have sex whenever they can – even when they shouldn't. They put love first. They celebrate romance in moonlight when the shop is closed.

Compare with
'Porphyria's Lover': the narrator desires Porphyria but in a different way.

Humour

Many of the mental pictures the narrator creates – his wife mocking his father, wearing a tartan sari – and some of the expressions comparing making love with 'rowing through Putney' are funny. The humour fuels the spirit of freedom and mischief in the poem.

Compare with
'Before You Were Mine': the narrator teases her mother with her observations and memories.

'Climbing My Grandfather'

DO IT!

Choose two more themes relevant to 'Singh Song!' and to Love and relationships.

For each theme, list one more poem that you could compare with 'Singh Song!'.

Briefly explain each of your choices.

Language

The poem is written **phonetically**: words are spelled as they would sound when spoken by a recent Indian immigrant. For example, 'he vunt [wants] me not to hav[e] a break.' This technique helps make the dramatic monologue more powerful because we can 'hear' the speaker. It helps us to imagine the lively personality that makes the narrative energetic and funny.

The words are not just written phonetically; they are also written in an Indian immigrant dialect rather than in Standard English. For example, the narrator tells us that 'Above my head high heel tap di ground.' In Standard English this would read, 'Above my head <u>a</u> high heel tap<u>s</u> the *<u>floor</u>*.' The grammar – and sometimes the vocabulary – differs between Standard English and Indian immigrant dialects. This method again helps Daljiit Nagra to let us *hear* the narrator and his customers. Look at how one student deals with this aspect of the poem:

> Daljiit Nagra has said that he is not trying to make fun of his narrator's voice, and he wants readers to 'see through their own prejudices' about accents. The phonetic spellings and the non-standard English in 'Singh Song!' make the narrator come to life for us and sound real, rebellious and funny!

Structure and form

The poem is a dramatic monologue brought to life by the authentic voices and the colourful details. The whole poem is structured like a song (as suggested by the title) and frustrated shoppers' words come in like a chorus. The poem slips in and out of rhythm to suit the narrator's changing mood – either fed up with the boring routines of work and customer demands, or buoyant with passion, romance and the dream of escape.

To suit the poem's 'up and down' emotions, rhymes come and go as well. Often they arrive suddenly and briefly to strengthen a moment of comedy, such as the rhyming of 'chutney' and 'Putney'.

Sometimes Nagra uses **assonance** (repeating vowel sounds) rather than full rhyme to make his poem infectiously 'singable'. In the second 'chorus' for example, assonance links 'bride' to 'cry', 'Singh' to 'bin' and 'date' to 'stale'.

Find and list two other examples in the poem of: **1** rhyme and **2** assonance.

See how one student refers to details in the poem to support their ideas about another aspect of the poem's structure.

> The poem's mood switches between despair and joy as the narrator thinks about his work, or his relationship with his wife. In stanza one he is bored with work; in stanza two he celebrates his secret passion. In stanza three the shoppers mock and accuse him; in stanza four he longs to join his wife again. The poem keeps switching emotionally, giving it the comic effect of a pantomime (Boo! Hooray!).

STRETCHIT!

Re-read the stanza beginning, 'late in di midnight hour'.

Explain how Daljiit Nagra uses rhyme and half rhyme for meaning and effect.

1. What does the narrator do when he has no customers?
2. What does he compare their lovemaking to?
3. What do his customers call him?
4. What is the narrator's religion?
5. List three things his customers complain about.
6. Where do the narrator and his wife sit after the shop has shut?
7. How does his wife offend his parents?
8. What does the narrator suggest by comparing his wife's eyes with guns?
9. How does Daljit Nagra help us to imagine the narrator and his personality?
10. Why does the narrator describe the stairs he and his wife come down at night as 'whispering'?

- Add your own annotations to the poem, exploring more of its details and their effects. Include the underlined words or phrases.
- Online you will find a copy of the poem with more detailed annotations.

AQA exam-style question

Compare how poets present excitement and/or a sense of adventure in 'Singh Song!' and in one other poem from Love and relationships.

[30 marks]

Climbing My Grandfather

Andrew Waterhouse (1958–2001)

I decide to do it free, without a rope or net.
First, the old brogues, dusty and cracked;
an easy scramble onto his trousers,
pushing into the weave, trying to get a grip.
By the overhanging shirt I change
direction, traverse along his belt
to an earth-stained hand. <u>The nails</u>
<u>are splintered and give good purchase,</u>
<u>the skin of his finger is smooth and thick</u>
<u>like warm ice</u>. On his arm I discover
the glassy ridge of a scar, place my feet
gently in the old stitches and move on.
At his still firm shoulder, I rest for a while
in the shade, not looking down,
for climbing has its dangers, then pull
myself up the loose skin of his neck
to a smiling mouth to drink among teeth.
Refreshed, I cross the screed cheek,
to stare into his brown eyes, watch a pupil
slowly open and close. Then up over
the forehead, the wrinkles well-spaced
and easy, to his thick hair (soft and white
at this altitude), reaching for the summit,
where gasping for breath I can only lie
<u>watching clouds and birds circle,</u>
feeling his heat, knowing
the slow pulse of his good heart.

Summary

The poem is about exploring your grandfather's life (grandparents are traditional objects of respect and admiration) in order to learn about and maybe even escape from your own past. There are risks – 'Climbing has its dangers' – that you might make discoveries you can't cope with yet, but at the end – at the 'summit' – risk-taking pays off.

The narrator (a child) launches straight into the adventure of climbing his grandfather as if he is a mountain. He is going to do this 'free' without any aids. (Notice the extended metaphor of rock climbing used throughout the poem. The narrator is, of course, not literally climbing, but is exploring his past and getting to know his grandfather.)

The narrator begins at ground level, with the shoes, before moving easily on to the 'trousers'. The 'overhanging shirt' is the first obstacle, but he manages this by moving sideways to the 'belt'. The 'nails' on the hand enable his grip before moving to the 'ridge' of a 'scar' and the 'shoulder'. (The narrator places his feet 'gently' on the scar showing his affection for his grandfather and what he represents.)

The narrator 'rests' before moving up the neck and 'mouth'. After a drink, crossing the cheek, he stares into the 'brown eyes' and moves over 'forehead' to the summit. The narrator watches the 'clouds and birds' as he catches his breath. (We are not told directly about the grandfather's character, but we can infer through the warm images used at the end of the poem, his smile and the 'good heart' suggesting that these discoveries and risks are helpful and worth taking).

STRETCH IT!

The grandfather wears shoes described as 'the old brogues'. What does this choice of shoe tell us about him literally and metaphorically? Link the reference to shoes to another poem in the Love and relationships cluster. How are shoes used to show character in both poems?

DEFINE IT!

altitude – (climbing term) the distance (height) between the top of the mountain and sea level

brogues – strong outdoor shoes with a distinctive pattern in the leather

free – (climbing term) climbing without using pegs and belays to help

glassy ridge – (climbing term) an icy, narrow section of a climb

overhanging – (climbing term) a section of rock where the top part sticks out over the bottom section

purchase – (climbing term) firm contact or grip

scramble – (climbing term) move over rough ground using hands and/or feet

summit – (climbing term) highest point of a hill or mountain

traverse – (climbing term) cross a rock face with sideways movements

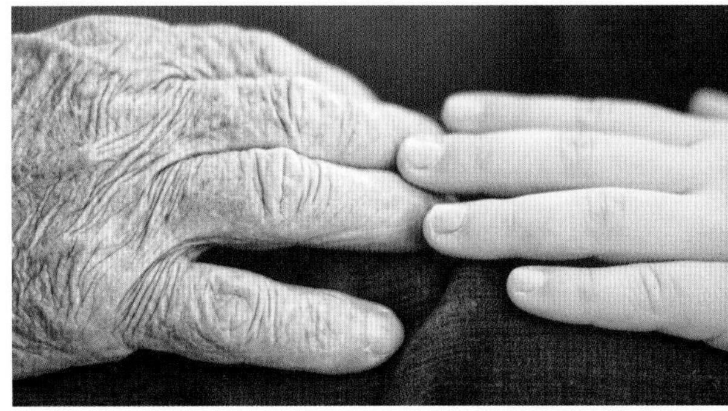

DO IT!

What clues are we given that the grandfather does physical work?

Context

Andrew Waterhouse was a keen environmentalist, interested in the natural world. In his obituary in *The Guardian* newspaper, his imagination was described as 'clear and uncluttered' and his poetic world is described as 'having nothing ordinary in it'.

Themes

Love: family ties

Exploration of the past through the extended metaphor of 'climbing' the grandfather reveals the links between the lives and experiences of our ancestors and our future.

Compare with
'Before You Were Mine': exploration and reimagining of the mother's past life.

Adventure/risk

The extended metaphor of climbing and mountaineering in the poem signals the adventure of discovering your past and all the 'cracks' and risks that you may encounter while doing so.

Compare with
'Love's Philosophy': persuasive argument built to coax the lover into risking the adventure of a kiss.

Nature and the natural world

The poem uses an extended metaphor of climbing and mountaineering to show the relationship between the narrator and his past. The grandfather is described as a mountain (suggesting power and grandeur). Birds and clouds are symbols of freedom and the future.

Compare with
'Sonnet 29 – "I think of thee!"': extended metaphor of a tree and a vine used to show loving thoughts.

Language

There are two groups of words in the poem: terms relating to climbing, 'free' climbing, 'an easy scramble', etc. and descriptions of the grandfather's physical presence, 'old brogues', the 'weave' of his 'trousers', etc.

The poem is affectionate in tone with a sense of wry humour. We are told that the narrator rests, 'not looking down/for climbing has its dangers'. The metaphorical meaning of this is darker. If we go searching into our past, it can be risky and fraught with 'dangers'.

Language choices are made to show the effort of climbing: he 'pushes' into the weave; he is 'trying' to grip. At the end of the climb he is 'gasping for breath' showing the physical challenge.

Look at one student's writing about the grandfather.

> The extended metaphor at the heart of the poem shows the reader the risks and 'dangers' of exploring the past, while at the same time reassuring the reader that this effort and 'gasping for breath' will pay off at the end. A metaphor for respect and admiration we give to past generations, the grandfather is studied as the narrator makes the journey to the 'summit'. once there, his risk-taking pays off as he recognises the grandfather's 'good heart' as he sees the 'birds' and 'clouds', symbols of his freedom, from the security of his grandfather's dependable platform.

Here the student is interpreting the poem by drawing on inferences made through the writer's language choices. This enriches their interpretation.

Structure and form

The poem is written in free verse as one long stanza representing the mountain – the grandfather – that the narrator climbs.

Ideas comparing the grandfather to the majesty of a mountainous landscape run throughout the poem. The climb begins at ground level – the shoes – and moves upwards until the summit is reached, complete with snow – thick hair ('soft and white/at this altitude'). This idea, running over two lines, imitates the physical challenge of reaching the summit.

The final lines of the poem are shorter, again replicating the physical shape of the mountain and the grandfather. The long vowel sounds in 'feeling his heat, knowing/the slow pulse of his good heart' imitate the slowing heart rate following rest after the exhilaration of the climb.

Complete the lists below with climbing vocabulary and physical descriptions of the grandfather from the poem. Continue on a separate piece of paper if necessary.

Climbing vocabulary	Physical descriptions of the grandfather
'I decide to do it free'	'old brogues'

1 Find three quotations to show what the grandfather was wearing.
2 What quotation tells us that the grandfather works on the land or in the garden?
3 How do we know that climbing is difficult for the narrator?
4 What is meant by a 'traverse'?
5 What can we infer by 'firm shoulder'?
6 What does the 'scar' suggest?
7 What could the 'birds and clouds' symbolise?
8 Find three quotations to show that the climb was hard.
9 Explain what you understand by 'warm ice'.
10 Why isn't the poem broken up into stanzas?

- Add your own annotations to the poem, exploring more of its details and their effects. Include the underlined words or phrases.
- Online you will find a copy of the poem with more detailed annotations.

AQA exam-style question

Compare how poets present family relationships in 'Climbing My Grandfather' and in one other poem from Love and relationships.

[30 marks]

Essentials

DO IT!

Re-read all the poems.

Note down how each one is relevant to the overall Love and relationships theme.

For example, in 'The Farmer's Bride' we are presented with a picture of an unequal relationship in which the farmer chooses, traps and imprisons his too-young bride. The result is a relationship that is distant, cold and unhappy, leaving the farmer with regrets. There is love, though: the wife loves animals and is trusted by them.

Themes

The overall theme for all these poems is Love and relationships. Don't lose sight of that: *love and relationships should be the 'focal point' of your study of all the poems*. The theme is quite broad: not all the poems are about romantic love – or even about romantic love 'gone wrong'. Family relationships are another clear focus. You see this in poems such as 'Eden Rock', 'Follower' and 'Climbing My Grandfather'.

NAIL IT!

Focus on the key element in the question.

Within the overall Love and relationships theme, your exam question will choose a specific key element such as marriage, parent/child relationships, breaking away, childhood memories, etc.

- Make sure you spot the key element in the question.
- Stay relevant to that key element throughout your answer.

Language

When you re-read the Love and relationships poems, notice any similarities in language style and methods, even if the poems come from different points in history. For example, 'Mother, any distance' uses an extended metaphor of a tape measure to explore the complex relationship between mother and son. In 'Sonnet 29 – "I think of thee!"' we see an extended metaphor used to show the lover as a sturdy tree with the narrator's loving (or obsessive) thoughts winding around him like vines.

Another example of shared language is the use of the names of real things and people to stir up a sense of nostalgia. This technique is used in two poems about family relationships: 'Eden Rock' refers to 'a Thermos' and an 'H.P. sauce bottle' while in 'Before You Were Mine', references to 'Marilyn' and the 'high-heeled red shoes' evoke the mother's glamorous but lost youth.

Other shared patterns of language you could explore include: images of cold/death in 'Winter Swans', 'Neutral Tones', 'When We Two Parted'; images from nature in 'Sonnet 29 – "I think of thee!"', 'Letters from Yorkshire', 'The Farmer's Bride', 'Love's Philosophy'.

DO IT!

Which poems make use of each of the following language features:

- plain, colloquial language
- references to the sun
- the creation of vivid and detailed visual images?

Structure and form

Think about how the structure and form of each poem help your understanding of its meaning and effect. The shape of 'Climbing My Grandfather' is cliff-like – tall and imposing. The sonnet form of 'Sonnet 29 – "I think of thee!"' is dense and formal – rather like the poem's central image of vines twining around a tree. 'The Farmer's Bride' and 'Singh Song!' both have looser forms with varied stanza lengths, but also a structure that suggests folk songs with choruses that listeners can join in with.

It is worth reading poems aloud and hearing the rhythms and sounds that give each poem a distinct pattern and coherence. We have already looked at the song-like qualities of two of the poems, but you will find that all the poems have their own distinctive sound. For example, 'Letters from Yorkshire' is broken into three-line stanzas, but mostly these breaks fall – unnaturally – in the middle of sentences. The shape and structure of the poem suggests difficult ideas coming to the narrator, who is trying to make sense of them for us. By contrast, 'Porphyria's Lover' reads slowly but evenly, the form suggesting the narrator's insane calmness, his confidence, his lethal sense of purpose.

Look back through all the poems:

- Read them aloud.
- Note down anything distinctive about patterns in them – repeated sounds and techniques.
- Find other poems that are similar in structure and form, and poems that contrast with them.

Read the notes on the structure and form of each poem in the previous pages. These will help you to make your own notes and to compare and contrast poems.

Context

The Love and relationships poems come from different times and cultures, and they are written by poets who have different attitudes and beliefs, and have had different personal experiences. Throughout society, attitudes towards love and relationships change constantly and so will opinions. This is what we mean by 'context': the circumstances that explain the tone and ideas in a poem. We mustn't forget that attitudes that might have been normal when a poem was written might be quite different from those that a modern reader brings to the poem.

NAIL IT!

By all means, allow what you know of a poem's context help you to write meaningfully about the key element given to you in your exam question. However, in general the best rule is to let the poem speak for itself: don't read too much into it by trying to make it explain aspects of the poet's life. Focus on *your* reaction to the poem and the methods the poet has used to create that reaction in you.

Doing well in your AQA exam

NAILIT!

- Your AQA exam question will name one Love and relationships poem and tell you to compare it with another Love and relationships poem of your own choice.
- The named poem will be printed on the paper.
- **Read the question before you read the named poem** so that you re-read the poem with the question focus in mind.
- Read the question carefully and understand it. Make sure you stay relevant to the question.

Understanding the question

Make sure you understand your exam question so that you do not include in your answer material that is irrelevant to what the question has asked.

Below is an AQA exam-style question. The question has been prepared by a student so that they fully understand it. Look at their notes.

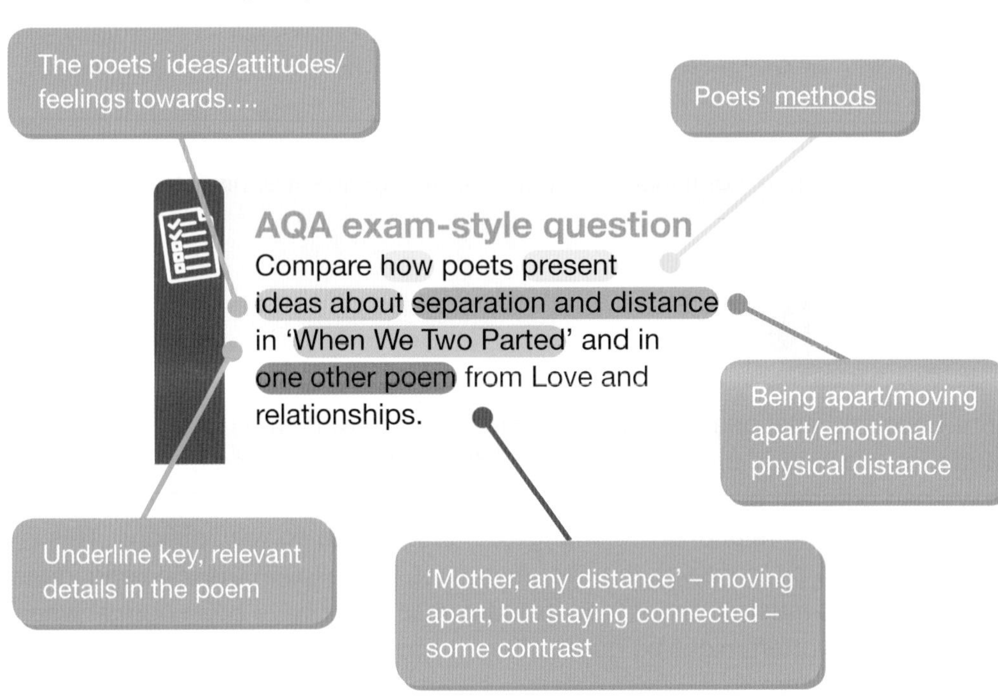

The poets' ideas/attitudes/ feelings towards....
Poets' methods
AQA exam-style question
Compare how poets present ideas about separation and distance in 'When We Two Parted' and in one other poem from Love and relationships.
Being apart/moving apart/emotional/ physical distance
Underline key, relevant details in the poem
'Mother, any distance' – moving apart, but staying connected – some contrast

This student has studied the question carefully and decided that:

- the focus is on separation/distance (mainly emotional)
- 'ideas about' includes the poets' attitudes and feelings (tone)
- 'Mother, any distance' is a good choice of comparison/contrast with the named poem.

'Pinning the question down' like this – making sure it is understood properly – has allowed the student to choose useful evidence to support their answer. In the examination room it is easy to misread questions, answering the question you hoped to see, rather than the one that is actually on the paper. Once you have prepared the question in the way shown above, you will be ready to re-read the named poem in the light of the question focus. As you read, underline relevant details.

Choose another question from earlier in this *AQA Study Guide*. Prepare the question as above.

Planning your answer

Once you have spent a couple of minutes 'pinning down' the question, planning your answer will be quite straightforward. Your brief plan should set out:

- your key, *relevant* ideas
- the content of each of four or five paragraphs
- the order of the paragraphs.

Practise planning as part of your revision programme.

Here is the same student's plan for their answer to the exam question on page 78:

NAILIT!

Spend 7–10 minutes on understanding the question, reading the named poem and planning your answer. There are no marks for using lots of words. Instead, you should aim to write enough *good*, *useful* words. Aim for four or five well-planned paragraphs (plus a brief introduction and conclusion).

<table>
<tr><th>Paragraph</th><th colspan="2">Content</th><th>Timing plan</th></tr>
<tr><td>1</td><td colspan="2">Introduction - use the question prep to establish focus of answer and my own choice of poem.</td><td>9.35</td></tr>
<tr><td>2</td><td colspan="2">Explore 'When We Two Parted' - evidence of separation/narrator's feeling</td><td>9.38</td></tr>
<tr><td>3</td><td>Distance in 'Mother' will never be total? Tension between freedom and 'pinch'</td><td rowspan="3">Refer back to question focus/wording.
Sometimes consider connotations of 'distance'.</td><td>9.45</td></tr>
<tr><td>4</td><td>Different formats - direct and literal address to lover ('WWTP'); metaphor based on real situation ('Mother')</td><td>9.52</td></tr>
<tr><td>5</td><td>Overall comparison of attitudes: breaking away exciting ('Mother'); looking back/blaming ('WWTP')</td><td>9.59</td></tr>
<tr><td>6</td><td colspan="2">Brief conclusion - which poet's ideas/feelings are more convincing for modern readers?</td><td>10.05</td></tr>
</table>

Sticking to the plan

Note how this student has jotted down time points for when they should move on to the next section of their answer. That way they make sure they do not get stuck on one point and fail to cover the question focus in enough breadth.

Go back to the exam question that you chose for the Do it! on pago 78. Dovolop a brief plan for it as above.

Planning to meet the mark scheme

The plan above suggests that the student knows what their examiner is looking for. (See the summary mark scheme on page 80.)

Assessment objective (AO)	What the plan promises
AO1 (Read, understand and respond)	Understanding of a number of ideas relevant to the main question focus – distance, being apart, as well as connection. Some personal interpretations to be included – suggested by the questioning of 'distance' in 'Mother'.
AO2 (Language, form and structure)	Exploring the poems will include close engagement with language/form, e.g. different formats – direct and literal ('When We Two Parted'), metaphor ('Mother'); and effects of language choices ('connotations').
AO3 (Context)	How readers in different times might react differently ('modern reader').

What your AQA examiner is looking for

Your answer will be marked according to a mark scheme based on three assessment objectives (AOs). The AOs focus on specific knowledge, understanding and skills. Together, the AOs are worth 30 marks, so it is important to understand what the examiner is looking out for.

Mark scheme

AQA will mark your answers in 'bands'. These bands roughly equate as follows:

- band 6 approx. grades 8 and 9
- band 5 approx. grades 6 and 7
- band 4 approx. grades 5 and 6
- band 3 approx. grades 3 and 4
- band 2 approx. grades 1 and 2.

Most importantly, the improvement descriptors in the table below will help you understand how to improve your answers and, therefore, gain more marks. The maximum number of marks for each AO is shown.

Assessment objective (AO)		Improvement descriptors				
		Band 2 Your answer…	**Band 3** Your answer…	**Band 4** Your answer…	**Band 5** Your answer…	**Band 6** Your answer…
AO1 (12 marks)	**Read, understand and respond**	supports simple comparisons between the poem with references to textual details.	sometimes explains comparisons between the poem in relation to the question.	clearly compares the poem in relation to the question.	develops a thoughtful comparison of the poem in relation to the question.	critically explores and compares the poem in relation to the question.
	Use evidence	makes some comments about these references.	refers to details in the poem to back up points.	carefully chooses close references to the poem to back up points.	thoughtfully builds appropriate references into points.	chooses precise details from the poem to make points convincing.
AO2 (12 marks)	**Language, form and structure**	mentions some of poets' methods.	comments on some of the poets' methods, and their effects.	clearly explains poets' key methods, and their effects.	thoughtfully explores poets' methods, and their effects.	analyses poets' methods, and how these influence the reader.
	Subject terminology	uses some subject terminology.	uses some relevant terminology.	helpfully uses varied, relevant terminology.	makes thoughtful use of relevant terminology.	chooses subject terminology to make points precise and convincing.
AO3 (6 marks)	**Contexts**	makes some simple inferences about contexts.	infers poets' points of view and the significance of contexts.	shows a clear appreciation of poets' points of view and the significance of contexts.	explores poets' points of view and the significance of relevant contexts.	makes perceptive and revealing links between the poem and relevant contexts.

AO1 Read, understand and respond/Use evidence

Make sure you read and answer your question carefully. Your examiner will be looking for evidence that you have answered the question given. Do not go into your exam with an answer in mind. Knowing the poems very well will give you the confidence to show your understanding of them and their ideas as you answer the question on the paper in front of you. You mustn't just show off your knowledge and understanding of the poems: you need to use that knowledge and understanding to answer the question thoughtfully.

Using evidence means supporting your ideas with well-chosen, relevant references to the poems. They can be indirect references – such as brief mentions of an idea or description in a poem – or direct references – quotations. Choose and use evidence carefully so that it really does support a point you are making. Quotations should be as short as possible, and the very best ones are often neatly built into your own writing.

AO2 Language, form and structure/Subject terminology

The language and structural features in a poem have been chosen carefully for effect. Good answers will not just point out good words a poet has used: they will explore the likely effects of those word choices on the reader.

Subject terminology is about choosing your words carefully, using the right words and avoiding vague expressions. It is also about using terminology *helpfully*. For example, here are two different uses of subject terminology in relation to the poem 'Walking Away', the first much more useful than the second:

Student answer A

'like a winged seed' is a simile that clearly suggests the boy's movement towards freedom, but also suggests to the reader that the boy's future is haphazard, subject to chance - just as a 'seed' can land anywhere.

Student answer B

'Like a winged seed' is a good simile.

AO3 Contexts

Notice the emphasis on '*relevant* contexts' higher up the mark criteria. Here are some useful questions to hold in your head when you refer to context:

- How might the society a poet lived in have influenced their ideas and attitudes?
- What beliefs and assumptions have influenced how you respond to a poem?
- How has comparing poems enriched your understanding of them?

The best answers will only include contextual information that is directly relevant to the question, not just the poem.

To boost your marks when answering questions, do the following:

- Know the poems well. Read and study them. Make up your own mind about them.
- Don't go into your exam with ready-made answers.
- Read the question and make sure you answer it thoughtfully.
- Choose details in the poems that will support your points.
- Always comment on the *effect* of details you choose.

Introductions and conclusions are not essential. Write them only if they help you to answer the question. However, it will help you organise your thinking if you mention your second, chosen poem in your introduction, and briefly outline some overall points of comparison (and/or contrast) between the two poems.

Student A's is the better introduction. Explain why. (Check the Nail it! advice on this page.)

Writing your answer

Getting started

You have looked at one student's plan, and you will have noticed that they have decided to write a short introduction. Here are the openings of two students' answers to the question on page 78: Compare how poets present ideas about separation and distance in 'When We Two Parted' and in one other poem from Love and relationships.

Student answer A

Byron's 'When We Two Parted' shows the emotional impact of separation and distance on a formerly loving relationship. In 'Mother, any distance', Simon Armitage also explores separation and distance. However, this emotional separation is shown within a parent/child relationship.

Student answer B

I am going to write about how two poets write about separation and distance. First, I am going to write about 'When We Two Parted' which was published in 1816 then I am going to talk about 'Mother, any distance' which was published in 1993. This is a long time apart so they will understand distance differently. Those are the sorts of things I'm going to write about in my answer.

The response

Look at the student's plan for the essay on page 78. Here is part of paragraph two of that student's answer. Note the way they use quotations to closely examine relevant details of Byron's language choices. An examiner has made some comments in the margin.

Byron presents distance and separation when a love affair ends as being like a death. The 'half broken-hearted' narrator addressing his lover tells us, 'Pale grew thy cheek and cold'. This pallor of death, showing her emotional distance, is continued with 'colder thy kiss'. Here, the intimacy of a 'kiss' is infected by the death of the relationship. This extended metaphor of death continues as his heartbreak is compared to grief, 'In silence I grieve' and her name is 'A knell in my ear'. Byron links the end of the affair to the imposed separation that happens when someone dies. However, despite his grief, the narrator's sorrow at their separation is fuelled by bitterness, as he tells us 'long, long shall I rue thee' showing the reader that he regrets ever loving her.

The words of the question are used to clearly focus on what is being asked.

Direct evidence used – and built neatly into student's own words.

Using words from the question to keep on track.

Confident focus on writer's craft.

Effect of words is identified and analysed closely.

Paragraph topics

The rest of your paragraphs should each deal with a subtopic of the main focus of the question. Here, the question focuses on the poets' presentation of ideas about separation and distance. The student's plan suggests that the next three paragraph topics will be: an exploration of distance in 'Mother, any distance', then how different formats are used by the two poems, then an overall comparison of attitudes towards distance and separation. The 'overall comparison' paragraph will help the student to address the 'Compare how poets present' aspect of the question: in other words, the student can explore what each poet wanted the reader to learn and understand about distance and separation.

Below you will see how – in part of their 'overall comparison' paragraph – the same student makes reference to the poets' attitudes to distance and separation. This shows that the student understands that the poems are constructed to express ideas or sometimes a definite message. The references are underlined to point them out.

> Both poets present ideas about distance and separation but with contrasting attitudes. In 'Mother, any distance', Armitage shows the reader how breaking away - separation - can be exciting and full of promise. We see the narrator 'reach' towards the 'hatch' that leads to an 'endless sky' suggesting infinite possibilities. Even 'hatch', playing on the idea of a creature emerging from the protection of an egg, suggests the possibility of new and exciting experiences. In 'When We Two Parted' Byron presents a narrator who views the distance between himself and his lover as a focus for his blame and bitterness. He talks of her coldness towards him and predicts that if they were to meet in the future, despite not knowing how to 'greet' her, he knows he will continue to react with 'silence and tears'. Here, the narrator makes it clear that despite the distance between them, his love - and pain - will continue...

NAIL IT!

Key rules for writing a good answer:

- Understand and plan.
- Be aware of the mark scheme (see page 80).
- Answer the question, making clear and relevant points.
- Back up your points with evidence, including some short quotations.

Using evidence:

This student uses indirect evidence to make general references to ideas in the poem and uses direct evidence in the form of quotations when they know them. Both forms of evidence are valid.

Ending your answer

Don't worry about elaborate conclusions: if you have nothing more to say, then just stop. The answer we have been looking at just ends like this:

> Both poets show how separation and distance is a part of our lives and has been part of our lives throughout history. A modern reader understands the need to grow and distance ourselves from our parents. However, the reader also knows that it will cause heartbreak if we are not in control of the separation.

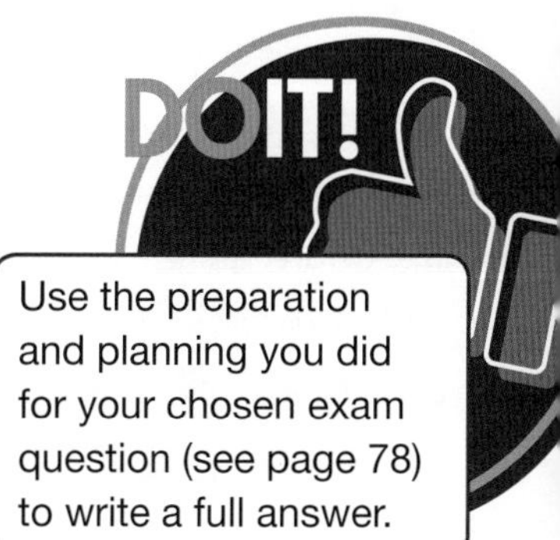

Use the preparation and planning you did for your chosen exam question (see page 78) to write a full answer.

Going for the top grades

Of course, you will always try to write the best answer possible, but if you are aiming for the top grades then it is vital to be clear about what examiners will be looking out for. The best answers will tend to:

• show a clear understanding of both the poem *and* the exam question • show insight into the poem and the question focus • explore the poem in relation to the focus of the question • choose evidence precisely and use it fluently	**AO1**
• analyse the writer's methods and their effect • use relevant, helpful subject terminology	**AO2**
• explore aspects of context that are relevant to the poems and question.	**AO3**

A great answer **will not** waste words or use evidence for its own sake.

A great answer **will** show that you are engaging directly and thoughtfully with the poem and the question, not just scribbling down everything you have been told about the poem.

The best answers will be RIPE with ideas and engagement:

R	• Relevant	Stay strictly relevant to the question.
I	• Insightful	Develop relevant insights into the poem, its structure and themes.
P	• Precise	Choose and use evidence precisely so that it strengthens your points.
E	• Exploratory	Explore relevant aspects of the poems, looking at them from more than one angle.

DO IT!

Find an essay or practice answer you have written about Love and relationships.

Use the advice and examples on this page to help you decide how your writing could be improved.

Below is a small part of a student's answer to the question about how poets present ideas about separation and distance in 'When We Two Parted' and 'Mother, any distance'. An examiner has made notes alongside.

What strikes me about Armitage's presentation of separating from his mother is that despite his need to break away from his mother, there is a true affection evident for her. He acknowledges that she is willing to 'help me' and the extended metaphor of objects tethered to a fixed point show the narrator as the object that has freedom to explore with the mother as the 'anchor'. The narrator in 'When we Two Parted' shows us a bleak and damaged view of separation. He is 'half broken-hearted' suggesting that one half of the partnership -the narrator - did not want the separation to happen. His bitterness is evident as he questions 'Why wert thou so dear?' yet admits that he will not tell of his love or sorrow even in the future as he would greet her with 'silence and tears'. This regret of the need for secrecy hits home for even a modern reader. The secrecy and deception at the heart of the relationship shown by 'Thy spirit deceive' causes the bitterness after their separation...

Clear and **nuanced** points.

Precise choice of evidence.

Good return to question focus to maintain relevance.

Precise evidence neatly integrated into the argument.

Separation and distance explored here.

Original insight based on context.

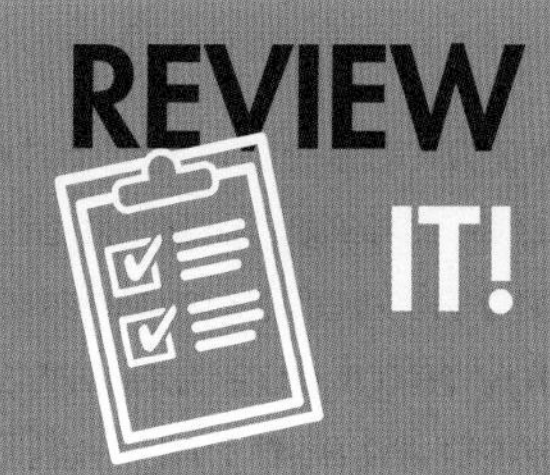

1 In your exam, how long should you give yourself to prepare, plan and write your Love and relationships answer?
2 What are the other two sections in Paper 2 Modern Texts?
3 How long should you spend planning and preparing your Love and relationships answer?
4 Why is it important to prepare or 'pin down' your exam question?
5 If you are in your exam and you find that you can't remember any direct quotations from your chosen poem, what can you do?
6 How many marks are AO1, AO2 and AO3 worth together?
7 Your friend has told you that they are going to learn an essay that they wrote in the mock exams as their revision. What would you say?
8 'Introductions and conclusions are not essential.' Is this true or false?
9 Create your own question by filling in the blanks:
Compare how poets present ______________ in ______________ and in one other poem from Love and relationships.
10 Plan a five-paragraph response to the question you created in question 9.

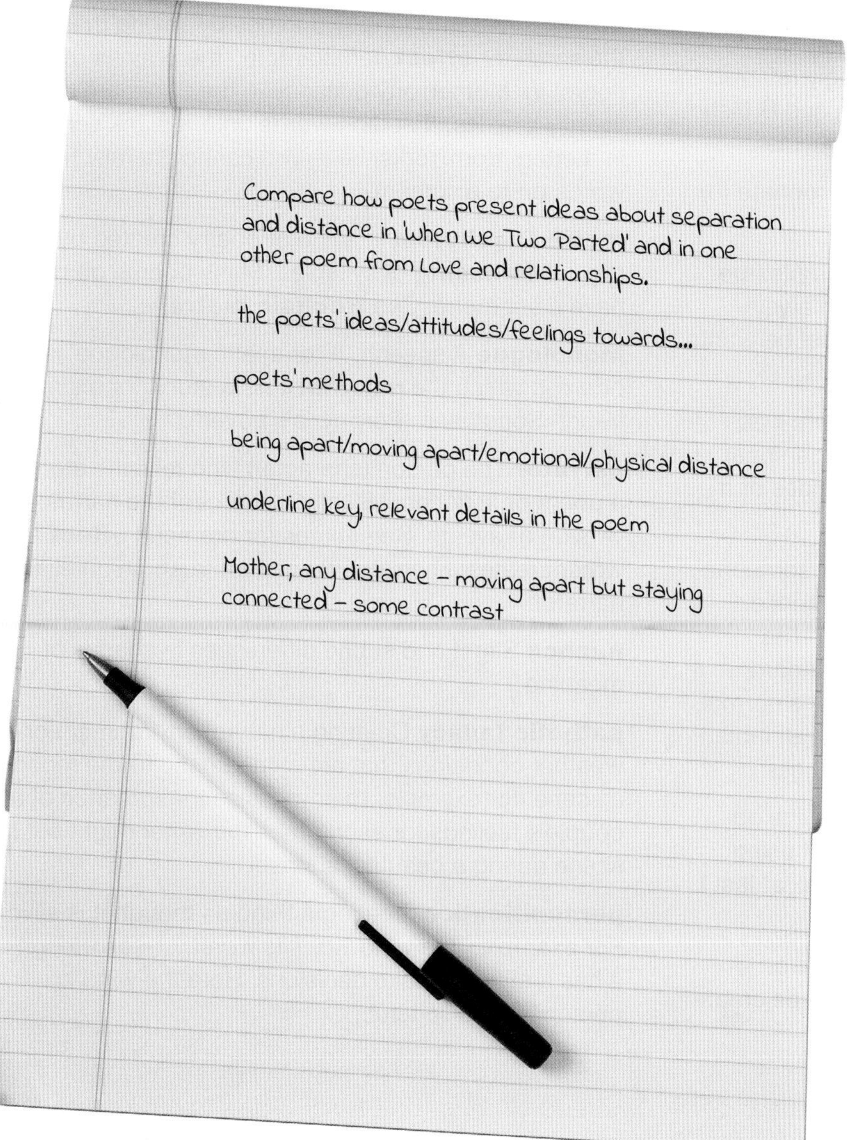

Compare how poets present ideas about separation and distance in 'When We Two Parted' and in one other poem from Love and relationships.
the poets' ideas/attitudes/feelings towards...
poets' methods
being apart/moving apart/emotional/physical distance
underline key, relevant details in the poem
Mother, any distance – moving apart but staying connected – some contrast

In the month leading up to your exam, all your revision should be based on planning and writing answers to exam questions. You will find plenty of exam questions in this guide for practice.

Glossary

adjective A word that describes a noun (for example: '*old* H.P. sauce bottle'; '*smooth white* shoulder').

allegory A **metaphor** extended throughout a text as a way of making a complex idea familiar and powerful (for example: the novel *Animal Farm* is a children's fable, which is widely understood as an allegory of the Russian Revolution and its aftermath. The swans' behaviour in the poem 'Winter Swans' is offered by Owen Sheers as an allegory of the problems and potential of human relationships).

alliteration Starting words that are close to each other with the same sound (for example: 'wrings with wrong' in 'Neutral Tones').

anaphora A repeated word or phrase to emphasise an idea.

assonance Repeating the vowel sound in a word (for example: 'span'/'hands'; 'leaving'/'unreeling' in 'Mother, any distance'). Assonance has been jokingly referred to as 'bad **rhyme**'. Contemporary American and British music tends to use assonance instead of rhyme.

colloquial Informal **language** that is appropriate for speech, but not usually for writing.

connotation An implied meaning (for example: the fact that Heaney says his father 'will not go away' rather than 'does not' connotes (implies) that he wants his father to go away).

context The circumstances in which a poem was written or is read. These could include the personal experiences of the poet, or the typical attitudes of a modern reader.

dialect The conventions that apply to how someone writes or speaks in order for them to make sense. Saying 'she runned' rather than 'she ran' in 'The Farmer's Bride' is a matter of dialect: in Standard English it is wrong; in some other dialects it is normal. 'Singh Song!' is unusual for being written in an Indian immigrant dialect rather than in Standard English.

enjambment Continuing the sense of one line on to the next. Usually, a writer does this by not using punctuation at the end of a line (for example: 'at last I knew/Porphyria worshipped me…').

effect The impact that a writer's words have on a reader: the mood, feeling or reaction the words create in the reader.

extended metaphor A **metaphor** that continues through several lines – or even a whole poem (for example: images relating to death in 'When We Two Parted').

iambic A type of **rhythm** which follows a pattern alternating between an unstressed and a **stressed** syllable (for example: 'The rain set early in to-night' in 'Porphyria's Lover').

iambic tetrameter A line of poetry that has eight syllables with a **stress** on the second, fourth, sixth and eighth syllables (see example in **iambic** above).

imagery Pictures in words. The main forms of imagery (other than description) are **similes** and **metaphors**.

language The words and the style that a writer *chooses* in order to have an **effect** on a reader.

metaphor Comparing two things by saying they are the same for **effect** (for example: 'the prairies of the floors' in 'Mother, any distance' – the floors are not literally prairies; 'Feeding words onto a blank screen' in 'Letters from Yorkshire' – you cannot literally feed words on to a screen).

metre The **rhythm** in a line of poetry created by the regular **stressing** of syllables. Many poems do not have a set metre. See **trochaic metre**.

monologue A speech. A 'dramatic monologue' is a poem in which the **narrator** tells a story (for example: 'Singh Song!' and 'Porphyria's Lover').

narrator The person (character) who tells the story in a poem or in fiction. Usually, we accept the narrator's version of events. Sometimes for dramatic **effect** a writer creates a narrator we cannot trust: an unreliable narrator.

nuance Slight and subtle differences in shades of meaning.

pathetic fallacy Creating a natural environment or weather conditions that are sympathetic to the mood of a scene (for example: to emphasise the romance of a couple's feelings for each other, the writer might set the scene during a beautiful sunrise).

personification Treating a thing as though it is alive. For example: 'the wind…*did its worst*…' – as though it has a mind to make decisions. Here the wind is personified as spiteful.

phonetic Written to show the pronunciation – the sound (for example: in 'Singh Song!' the **narrator** uses 'ven' for 'when', 'di' for 'the').

rhyme A line whose last **stressed** syllable has the same sound as a nearby line ending (for example: 'eyes'/'surprise' in 'Porphyria's Lover'). If the stressed syllable is not the last syllable in a line, then any following syllables must rhyme too (for example: *biscuit/risk it*).

rhyming couplet Two lines in a row that **rhyme** together.

rhythm The 'beat' of a line of poetry. Rhythm comes from the way the **stresses** (or 'beats') 'fall', or, more likely, are placed, by the poet. If the stresses fall at regular intervals, we say that the line has a 'regular rhythm'.

simile Comparing two things using 'like' or 'as' (for example: 'flying like a hare'; 'shy as a leveret' in 'The Farmer's Bride'.

stanza Another word for verse. Verse is normally used for songs, stanza for poetry.

stress Emphasis that falls on certain syllables to create a beat or **rhythm**.

structure The way a poem is organised so that it is coherent. The structure of a poem is its shape, its patterns of **imagery**, the sequence of its ideas.

trochaic metre A line of poetry which alternates between **stressed** and unstressed syllables, beginning with stressed (for example: 'Nothing in the world is single' in 'Love's Philosophy'). See **metre**.

verb A doing, being or having word (for example: to walk, to be or to have). Verbs change their form to show present (*walk*), past (*walked*) or future (*will walk*).